IN SEARCH OF THE
PRIME QUADRANT

THE QUEST FOR BETTER INVESTMENT DECISIONS

MO LIDSKY, IAN ROSMARIN,
JEREMY ROSMARIN, SETH WASSYNG

All rights reserved. No part of this book shall be reproduced or transmitted in any form or by any means, electronic, mechanical, magnetic, photographic including photocopying, recording or by any information storage and retrieval system, without prior written permission of the publisher. No patent liability is assumed with respect to the use of the information contained herein. Although every precaution has been taken in the preparation of this book, the publisher and author assume no responsibility for errors or omissions. Neither is any liability assumed for damages resulting from the use of the information contained herein.

Copyright © 2012 by Mo Lidsky, Ian Rosmarin, Jeremy Rosmarin, and Seth Wassyng

Prime Quadrant® is a registered trademark of Prime Quadrant LP.

ISBN 978-0-7414-7972-3 Paperback
ISBN 978-0-7414-7973-0 eBook
Library of Congress Control Number: 2012916489

Printed in the United States of America

Published October 2012

∞

INFINITY PUBLISHING
1094 New DeHaven Street, Suite 100
West Conshohocken, PA 19428-2713
Toll-free (877) BUY BOOK
Local Phone (610) 941-9999
Fax (610) 941-9959
Info@buybooksontheweb.com
www.buybooksontheweb.com

Dedicated to our loving families that have allowed us to share this work with you

"An investment in knowledge pays the best interest."

- Benjamin Franklin

Table of Contents

Introduction: How We Got Here	1
1. The Six Most Common Investment Mistakes	7
2. Apples and Oranges: Product vs. Process	27
3. Inefficient Markets: The Secrets of Outperformance	45
4. Risky Business: Capitalizing on Uncertainty	61
5. Spreading the Wealth: An Introduction to Asset Allocation	87
6. Knowing What You've Got: Defining the Asset Classes	101
7. The Art and Science of Manager Selection	119
8. The Death of the Insurance Dodo and Alternative Risk-Free Strategies	143
9. Getting A Good Night's Sleep: Mastering the Psychology of Investing	153
Appendix A	175
Appendix B	179
Endnotes	

About the Authors

IAN G. ROSMARIN, CA CIMA CLU TEP

Ian is the founder and principal of Prime Quadrant LP. He has been assisting wealthy families with their financial strategies, investing and structuring for over 30 years.

A graduate of the University of the Witwatersrand, Johannesburg, Ian placed first in the South African Institute of Chartered Accountants' Final Qualifying Examination in Auditing. Ian is a member of the Institute of Chartered Accountants of Ontario, a Certified Investment Management Analyst, a Chartered Life Underwriter and a member of the Society of Trust and Estate Practitioners.

Ian has a distinguished track record as an entrepreneur, having successfully established, purchased, run and sold several businesses. He was a senior officer in the world's largest company serving in-office health-care practitioners, where he established Henry Schein Financial Services and was responsible for the practice management software division, which serves more than 50,000 professional health-care practices in the United States.

Ian is active in the community as a board member of two sizable, Toronto-based, charitable foundations and an Alberta-based chartered trust company. He is the chair of the investment committee of a third, sizable, charitable foundation for a renowned international educational institution.

MO LIDSKY, BA M.SC MBA

Mo is a principal at Prime Quadrant LP. Prior to joining Prime Quadrant, Mo spent his career as a social entrepreneur, balancing the growth of his commercial ventures and his passionate involvement with non-profits.

Mo was the co-founder and owner of TMX Inc., a group of automobile restoration companies in Northeast Ohio, Founding Vice-President of CharityBids LLC, an online auction platform serving the non-profit sector, and the Chairman of FundCoaches Inc., a virtual fund-raising institute, and founding partner of Apex Global Capital, a microfinance company in the Caribbean.

Philanthropically, Mo spent five years as the national director and chief executive officer of Yeshiva University (Canada), Chairman of the THJ Foundation, and is still active on the boards of several non-profit organizations. He is currently completing a book on the sector, profiling Canada's 100 most generous philanthropists, entitled *The Philanthropic Mind*.

Mo holds multiple degrees, Magna Cum Laude, in Economics and Psychology, from Yeshiva University, and has an MBA from the University of Toronto's Rotman School of Management.

SETH WASSYNG, BBA

Seth is a principal at Prime Quadrant LP. Prior to joining Prime Quadrant, Seth worked at Scotia Capital on the trading floor in the Energy Derivatives group and at Dundee Wealth with the Project Management team.

Seth received a Bachelor of Business Administration (Honors) at the Schulich School of Business and has passed all three levels of the CFA program and may be eligible for the CFA charter upon completion of the required work experience.

JEREMY ROSMARIN, BA

Jeremy is an analyst at Prime Quadrant. He was a consultant for McGill University's Teva Initiative, for which he was awarded the Catalyst Award for Applied Student Research in 2012. Jeremy was Vice President of Finance for The McGill Foreign Affairs Review and STAND McGill.

Jeremy has a B.A. in Economics with Distinction from McGill University. He is a CFA level 3 candidate.

Acknowledgement

We are deeply grateful to our young associates, Jonathan Lax, Yoni Grunbaum and Yael Klein, for their immense contribution to this work. Their tireless efforts in researching, formatting, editing, and coordinating the logistics of production were invaluable. This book could not have been completed without them.

We would also like to recognize the following individuals, in alphabetical order, for their contribution in editing and reviewing this book: Howard English, Melanie Levcovich, Rose Lidsky, Allan Phillips, Stuart Schipper and Rachel Wertheimer. Thank you for your insights and feedback in refining the fruit of our labour.

We cannot possibly cite all the scores of authorities and sources consulted in the preparation of this book. To do so would require more space than is available. The list would include fund managers, co-investors, service providers, departments of various governments, libraries, periodicals and many individuals. We are deeply grateful to each of you for your contributions.

Disclaimer

This book is designed to provide information on investing best practices for high-net-worth families and individual investors. It is sold with the understanding that the publisher and author are not engaged in rendering any legal or accounting professional services. If legal or other expert assistance is required, the services of a competent professional should be sought.

It is not the purpose of this book to provide all of the information that is otherwise available to authors and/or publishers, but instead to complement, amplify and supplement other texts. You are urged to read all of the available material, learn as much as possible about your investment options, and tailor the information to your individual needs.

The ideas in this book do not provide any get-rich-quick schemes. Anyone who decides to pursue a course of action consistent with the ideas presented in this book must expect to invest considerable time and effort into it.

Every effort has been made to make this book as complete and as accurate as possible. However, there *may be mistakes*, both typographical and in content. Therefore, this text should be used only as a general guide and not as the ultimate source of investing information. Furthermore, this book contains information on investing best practices that is current only up to the printing date.

The purpose of this book is to educate and entertain. The authors and Prime Quadrant LP shall have neither liability nor responsibility to any person or entity with respect to any loss or damage caused, or alleged to have been caused, directly or indirectly, by the information contained in this book.

"All achievements, all earned riches, have their beginning in an idea."

- Napoleon Hill

Introduction
How We Got Here

How did we get here?

In 1997, Prime Quadrant's founder, Ian Rosmarin, retired from Henry Schein Inc., now a Fortune 500 company based in Long Island, N.Y., as President of the Technology and Financial Services Group. His stock and options in the company vested and he returned to living full-time, with his family, in Toronto.

Ian spent the rest of that year trying to get assistance in managing his family's nest egg and wanted to have it structured in the way leading pension plans and university endowments were organized. He soon realized that such help was not available in Canada for portfolios of his size. He therefore set out to do it himself. Before long, he met someone who fell in love with his approach, and asked for his help in replicating a similar investment plan. Reluctantly, Ian agreed. Without knowing it then, this fellow became Ian's first client, and Prime Quadrant was born.

Why is the model used by leading pension plans and university endowments so interesting?

For starters, the long-term returns achieved by these institutions have been (and continue to be) exceptional. Their investment officers have earned returns in the mid to high teens over the course of decades and have provided their organizations with unparalleled fiscal freedom and security. This level of performance results largely from their ability to invest in a highly diversified portfolio which includes many different asset classes. These asset classes include publicly traded stocks and bonds, private equity, private debt and real assets (such as real estate, commodities, and infrastructure projects), within many different types of investment structures, such as hedge funds and various investment partnerships.

While this asset allocation may be relatively simple to understand, it is difficult to implement for several reasons. First of all, investing in these assets often requires larger commitments than most private investors can and should make (some requiring as much as $5 million to $10 million per position). The investment providers do not generally want to deal with unsophisticated investors and often screen their clients based on the amount of money they can invest. Moreover, to effectively manage risk, investments in these asset classes require deep analysis and extensive experience. This process is labour-intensive and requires a far greater level of curiosity, and ability to satisfy that curiosity, than implementing traditional asset allocations. It also requires a great deal of investor education to ensure that clients will remain comfortable and committed to their profoundly different looking portfolios, regardless of possible short-term setbacks. Taxes for private investors must also be taken into consideration.

Is all this extra work, effort, complexity and, presumably, expense worth it?

We believe that a healthy portfolio should have numerous moderately sized positions, in the 2% to 5% range. This could be as many as 20 to 50 positions, all carefully customized and hand-picked to mesh with the needs and goals of the client.

Starting from the premises that the future is uncertain and that there is always a risk that something may go wrong, positions have to be large enough to be worth taking but not large enough to cause severe pain if lost entirely.

These portfolios require considerably more explanation, discussion and understanding as compared to traditional portfolios. This is one reason why, as part of our investment process, we meet with our clients on a regular basis (preferably, at least once a month).

The results from these efforts speak for themselves. During a period in which equities and "risk assets" were flat (at best), our reference portfolio, which has been managed according to our research since January 1st, 2000, achieved consistently high single-digit/low double-digit returns, compounded, net of all fees and expenses.

Just as important as the percentage return on this portfolio, is *how* the performance was achieved. Our reference portfolio contains only a small allocation to investment-grade credit securities, which have, over the same period, enjoyed an unprecedented (and possibly unrepeatable) bull market. Our returns are not a product of catching a rising tide which raised all boats but, rather, the investment philosophy described in this book, which applies across time and market environments.

Striving to create this type of portfolio is reflected in our name. The "Prime Quadrant" is the area on a risk-return graph where risk is lower and return is higher. We focus our research only on investments which fit into this profile and work alongside our clients to ensure that their specific needs are accounted for in the process.

Prime Quadrant Reference Account *(Net of fees)*	9.8%	$1 on Jan. 1st 2000 was worth $2.93 on June 30th, 2011
S&P 500 *(Gross of fees)*	0.90%	$1 on Jan. 1st 2000 was worth $1.11 on June 30th, 2011
MSCI World Index *(Gross of fees)*	1.70%	$1 on Jan. 1st 2000 was worth $1.21 on June 30th, 2011
HFRI Equity Hedge *(A well-known hedge fund index. Net of fees)*	5.66%	$1 on Jan. 1st 2000 was worth $1.88 on June 30th, 2011
S&P TSX 60 *(Gross of fees)*	6.06%	$1 on Jan. 1st 2000 was worth $1.97 on June 30th, 2011
Barclays Aggregate Bond Index *(a well-known investment grade bond index. Gross of fees)*	6.31%	$1 on Jan. 1st 2000 was worth $2.02 on June 30th, 2011

With superior risk-adjusted results and a higher sleep-at-night quotient that comes from diversification, our clients share a very high level of satisfaction and comfort. This satisfaction, we believe, is something that all high-net-worth individuals and families should share: That is why we embarked on writing this book.

Our approach is not for everyone, nor is it rocket science. That being said, we believe that, by following the best practices discussed in the chapters ahead, you will be well on your way toward making better investment decisions and achieving your personal goals.

"Investing is simple. It's just not easy."
- Warren Buffett

Chapter One
The Six Most Common Investment Mistakes

Our experience has shown that, for many wealthy families, managing their wealth can be more daunting than making money in the first place. The average investor's portfolio was flat to down over the first ten years of this millennium. The S&P 500 returns from 2000 to 2010 show a lost decade in which the equity market oscillated between elated and apocalyptic, only to settle around ambivalent. Volatility, and the uncertainty that comes with it, only increased in 2011 and as a result wealthy families have begun asking important questions with greater regularity.

In the wake of these recent developments, we will outline some of the common mistakes that wealthy families make and what they can do to avoid these mistakes moving forward. Many of the ideas expressed briefly in this chapter are discussed in more detail throughout this book. Understanding where one's family wealth is vulnerable to missteps can be the first important move for those looking to relieve some of the mental stress caused by their investing.

1. Skipping the Strategy

Reactionary vs. Strategic Investing

Many wealthy individuals are reactionaries in their investment process. Over the course of several years, they will allocate money to investments which seem, at any given moment in time, attractive. Although some people do well investing in attractive opportunities as they arise, the vast majority of individuals are better off investing strategically and creating a roadmap *before* investing. These investors can then let the roadmap guide their investment process rather than chase opportunities.

Through strategic investing, individuals can set guidelines about asset allocation, risk tolerance, liquidity, tax efficiency and other criteria to make sure that each subsequent investment they make is part of their overall life planning.

The main problem with reactionary investing is that, in its lack of process, the relationship between each investment is not sufficiently considered because each decision is made in isolation from the next. Investing in *reaction* to opportunities causes investors to very quickly lose sight of the forest for the trees.

An investment portfolio is much more than the sum of its individual parts. For example, the way in which investments interact with one another is very important. Specifically, strategic investing should take into consideration investors':

- *Ability* and *willingness* to take on risk.
- Liquidity and income requirements.
- Return objectives, in light of personal, familial and philanthropic goals.
- Time horizon, as a result of age and the ages of successors.
- Tax consequences.

- Legal restrictions.
- Unique circumstances or preferences, arising from the infinite characteristics which distinguish individuals from one another.

Unfortunately, many individuals and families do not consider all of these issues before investing their money and end up being disappointed or frustrated by the results. As Adam Smith once said, *"If you don't know who you are, the market is an expensive place to find out."*

The Investment Policy Statement

To address this issue, arguably the most important single document for wealthy families and their advisors is the investment policy statement (IPS). The IPS is the "investment constitution," which should be completed *prior to* an asset allocation plan. It outlines the client's needs and the rules which govern the investment portfolio. It sets guidelines for a client's asset allocation, liquidity and risk exposure. It also describes the process for updating these guidelines as the client's personal circumstances change over time. It strives to bring to fruition the benefits of strategic investing.

A good IPS is not a luxury – it is a necessity. Clients need to formalize their risk-return objectives and investment professionals need to understand exactly where their clients are coming from.

Without having a detailed, practical and strategic discussion before investing, client and advisor may as well be tethered together in a forest without a map for their entire relationship.

The valuable information contained in the IPS should not be flushed out over the course of years. It needs to be discussed at the outset between client and advisor and used as the basis for asset allocation. Clients, for their part, should demand this service from their advisors.

> *When one has finished building one's house, one suddenly realizes that in the process one has learned something that one really needed to know in the worst way - before one began.*
>
> -Friedrich Nietzsche

Revamping a Reactionary Portfolio

It is never too late to start investing more strategically. Whether an investment portfolio needs to be merely tweaked or strategically reallocated in its entirety, improving your investment strategy will always be helpful. In cases where a portfolio needs to be significantly reallocated, advisors and clients can work together to make the transition as undisruptive as possible.

2. Confusing 'Carpenters' with 'General Contractors' in Investing

In construction, the difference between a carpenter and a general contractor is clear to most people. A carpenter is a craftsperson – a person who is responsible for carrying out the physical tasks required to build a structure. A contractor is an overseer – a person who is responsible for making sure that the craftspeople are working well individually and as a unit. In construction, both roles are important, but each is clearly distinguished from the other.

In the investment management industry, the distinction between the "craftspeople" and the "contractors" often gets muddled. Investment *managers* are often given the role of carrying out investment tasks and at the same time overseeing their own work. Without oversight, different managers responsible for different portions of a person's net worth do not work as a cohesive unit.

Many families manage their wealth in a way that is analogous to them building a house with only craftspeople and no professional oversight. General contractors, project managers, architects, designers – all these roles are absent in the building of their financial estate. As a result, their investment managers have insufficient oversight and are strategically disconnected from one another.

These families would be better served if they had an advisor who would monitor the performance of individual investment managers to make sure each manager is performing according to their mandate and in a way which complements the others. In situations where a manager does not perform as expected, this advisor could recognize the situation and guide the client in a better direction.

3. Tolerating Conflicts of Interest

Confusing Products with a Process

Far too often, especially in Canada, clients are offered investment products rather than an investment process. For example, many investments which are recommended to clients by their advisor are developed (and incentivized to sell) in-house, so the "advisor" is also in essence a salesperson for their firm. In addition to this conflict of interest, recipients of product-based financial advisory are also unable to receive advice that is customized to their particular situation because their options are so limited.

In contrast to a professional who sells products, an advisor who offers a *process* will not be inclined to impose investments onto his or her clients. Instead, the advisor will, along with the client, develop guidelines and a philosophy for investing which will frame the investment decisions over time and help to identify opportunities accordingly. The range of options available to such an advisor's client is as infinite as the advisor's willingness to research.

Clients who are served products from a list are ultimately receiving a service designed for somebody else (or no one in particular). Conversely, process-based investment consulting or advisory services involve the creation of an investment mandate in accordance with each client's particular needs.

Following the Money Trail

Part of the product vs. process distinction is recognizing where investment professionals make their money from. "Advisors" who offer products rather than a process may receive all or part of their compensation for offering certain investments over others. This fee structure is wrought with conflicts of interest.

Wealthy individuals and families are best off with a trusted advisor who gets his or her income from only one place: the clients. Part of offering a process instead of products is limiting non advisor-client compensation and, when applicable, forwarding all tertiary fees right back to the clients.

4. Delusion of Diversification

Confusing Volatility with Risk

Most clients correctly understand that diversification among investments can decrease the volatility of a portfolio.

Diversification is also important, however, for reducing the risk of permanently losing capital.

Limiting volatility is very important for clients who, understandably, do not feel comfortable seeing the value of their investments decrease over a short period of time. We all need to sleep at night, and highly volatile returns certainly do not help most people get their rest.

Permanently losing capital, however, constitutes a different, more concerning, level of risk. Whereas some people are willing to sacrifice consistency for higher returns, no one in their right mind is comfortable irreparably harming their savings.

Diversification needs to focus not merely on limiting volatility to a range within which the investor can feel comfortable, but, more importantly, limiting the likelihood of some extreme negative event which can irrevocably harm a portfolio and its beneficiaries.

Diversification is also very important for reducing the degree to which one's investments are subject to the whims of any one asset class market (i.e. real estate, fixed income or equities). Dependency on a single market creates tremendous uncertainty of returns over any given decade. Although some investors are able and willing to live with such uncertainty, the majority are not. For this majority, diversification is very useful for making returns more predictable and sensitive to their spending needs, whether personal, corporate or philanthropic.

Asset Class Diversification

Diversification requires much more than just holding a large number of investments in a portfolio. In order to benefit from diversification – lowering volatility and decreasing the chance of permanently losing money, for a given investment return – investors should diversify across asset classes.

Common asset classes include: equities, real estate, investment-grade bonds, hedge funds, private equity, distressed debt and many others, including domestic and international versions of each. Although investments within asset classes tend to behave similarly to one another, investments across asset classes tend to behave differently.[1]

This relationship (correlation) among the investments is very important and useful. For example, if the stock market takes a turn for the worse, it is useful to have an investment which will increase in value in such a situation and offset the losses on the rest of a portfolio. Over time, investors who are properly diversified receive what is often called "the only free lunch in finance" – a higher level of returns for a given amount of volatility and uncertainty.

Most people have exposure to too few asset classes and are missing out on this free lunch. For example, the traditional 60% equity, 40% bond portfolio diversifies across just two asset classes.

Moreover, there is often an overlap between the equity and bonds in the portfolio, which happens when both the equity and the bonds are in the same type of companies (i.e. large-cap North American). This overlap mitigates the benefits of diversifying because the two asset classes will react similarly as events unfold.

For this reason, most institutional investors, such as pension funds and Ivy League endowments, have moved away from traditional asset allocations. Over the past two decades, they have shifted towards investing in alternative asset classes such as private equity, real estate, infrastructure, distressed securities, and various hedge fund strategies. Private investors who are able to do the same would be well served to do so.

Preparing for the Unprecedented

Mark Twain once, rather cynically, pointed out, *"October: This is one of the peculiarly dangerous months to speculate in stocks. The others are July, January, September, April, November, May, March, June, December, August and February."* Individuals were often told by their investment advisors during The Great Recession that extreme negative returns were acceptable because "the events of the time were unforeseeable." The whole point of diversification, however, is that investors should be protected from the unforeseeable.

Events are constantly unfolding in ways which are new and filled with uncertainty. One of the most important investing maxims is therefore: the one thing we know for sure is that we do not know what the future will bring. An investment advisor should understand that the future can bring with it unprecedented and unforeseeable events. Only with this understanding in mind can he or she craft a well-armored, properly diversified portfolio.

It was the lack of proper diversification across the investment gamut, combined with the financial leverage employed by managers, who were overly confident of their expected returns, which led to such extensive financial losses between 2006 and 2009. Many investment managers modeled their portfolios based on historical information, and were not prepared for the unprecedented. Many of them did not institute sufficient safeguards in their portfolios, and suffered tremendous losses because of the unforeseeable events that unfolded.

Good investors must always approach their process with wariness and humility, expecting what is often unexpected and preparing for worst-case scenarios. As the common refrain goes, *"Successful investors realize that 'get rich quick' usually means 'get poor quicker.'"*

5. Limited Investment Opportunities

One of the most significant mistakes many wealthy individuals make in their wealth management, particularly in Canada, is that they accept a limited range of investment options. High-net-worth investors have specific circumstances which warrant asset diversification different from that of the general population. For example, high-net-worth individuals typically have:

- The means to hire a professional to spend more time developing a strategic investment allocation.
- The legal qualifications required to invest in alternative investments, such as being categorized as Accredited Investors, for those who have investible assets in excess of $1 million, or Permitted Clients, who have investable assets of $5 million or more.
- Less need for investment liquidity because they can cover their living expenses with a smaller proportion of their wealth.

These characteristics of high-net-worth clients warrant having asset allocations which can be less liquid, more work-intensive and slightly more complex than those of other portfolios, resulting in higher risk-adjusted returns.

Alternative Investments

Alternative Investments – which consist of real assets, absolute return assets and private equity – fall into the category of being less liquid, more work-intensive and slightly more complex. When approached properly, such assets can provide investors with higher risk-adjusted returns. For reasons that we discuss in Chapters Five and Six, Alternative investments can be incredibly useful for investors who have the propensity to allocate to them. Unfortunately, the Canadian wealth management industry has lagged behind its global counterparts in offering its clients access to these opportunities.

Investors can be compensated for accepting a number of limitations. Two of these limitations include illiquidity and extended maturities. Since high-net-worth investors, generally, have more flexibility on liquidity and maturity than average investors do, they can get disproportionate compensation if they capitalize on their unique situation as investors.

Unfortunately, since many high-net-worth clients are not provided with sufficient access to alternative investments, they are insufficiently compensated for having more flexibility.

This liquidity and maturity flexibility is one of the reasons why university endowments, which have indefinite time horizons, have been able to maintain large pools of alternative assets and outperform other investors.

Learning from the Smart Money

The Ivy League university endowment funds are widely regarded as some of the most sophisticated investors in the world, particularly since strongly rebounding in 2009 and 2010 from their financial crisis lows.

The next graph shows a comparison of the returns from all endowments with those of the Ivy League endowments. From 1994 to 2005, Ivy Leaguers outperformed other endowments by over 3% per year. To put this outperformance into perspective, **on a portfolio with a starting value of $10 million, this superior return would yield an *additional $12 million* in wealth over ten years compared to the S&P 500. Compared to the performance of the average 65% equity 35% bond portfolio, the return would yield an *additional $19 million* in wealth over 10 years.**

Year	All Return	All Benchmark	Ivy League Return	Ivy League Benchmark
1994	5.8%	-1.1%	8.5%	-0.1%
1995	16.1%	16.2%	16.4%	17.2%
1996	19.7%	16.6%	24.4%	19.6%
1997	21.5%	21.4%	24.6%	21.4%
1998	18.6%	20.9%	19.1%	21.0%
1999	10.4%	15.8%	11.9%	16.2%
2000	20.2%	15.9%	26.8%	24.1%
2001	-2.9%	-8.9%	2.4%	-7.3%
2002	-4.5%	-12.1%	-0.8%	-11.5%
2003	4.6%	0.2%	9.1%	0.2%
2004	17.3%	11.3%	19.5%	10.0%
2005	13.1%	6.1%	16.9%	6.9%
Mean	11.7%	8.5%	14.9%	9.8%

Source: Lerner, Josh, Antoinette Schoar, and Jialan Wang. 2008. "Secrets of the Academy: The Drivers of University Endowment Success." *Journal of Economic Perspectives*

The Ivy League school endowments, over this same period of time, allocated a particularly high proportion of their portfolios to alternative investments. The following graph compares the alternative asset allocations of endowments under different categories. The best performing endowments, those of the Ivy Leagues, tend to invest more heavily in alternative investments.

Alternative Asset Allocation by School Type and Year (Median fraction of total assets invested in alternative asset classes, including hedge funds, venture capital and private equity)

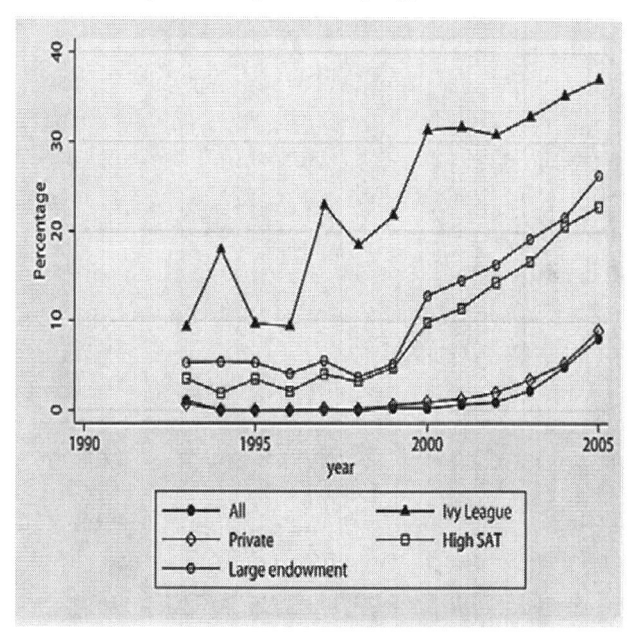

Source: Lerner, Josh, Antoinette Schoar, and Jialan Wang. 2008. "Secrets of the Academy: The Drivers of University Endowment Success." *Journal of Economic Perspectives*

Alternative investments are likely one driver of outperformance for these exceptional funds. **Even if we cannot determine the degree to which Alternative investments account for their superior returns, it is telling that the endowment portfolio managers who form, arguably, the most successful group of investors in the world, choose to allocate higher proportions of their assets under management to alternative investments.** Wealthy families would be well served to learn from these endowment fund managers and, in doing so, strive for access to a far greater range of investment opportunities than they currently have.

6. Weak Performance Evaluation

The renowned author and management guru, Peter Drucker, is often credited with coining the expression, *"If you cannot measure it, you cannot manage it."* He was 100% correct. In investing, there are many different numbers and metrics used to measure or evaluate performance. These include the annualized return, the internal rate of return, the cumulative return in percentage terms and cumulative return in dollar terms. These are just a sampling of the more popular measures. **The general rule of thumb is that certain performance measurements are better than others, but no single performance measurement can paint a complete picture.**

Annualized Return vs. Internal Rate of Return (IRR)

Two of the most popular performance measurement figures are the annualized return and the IRR. These two figures are referred to as the time-weighted return and the money-weighted return respectively. The annualized return ("time-weighted return") is simply the average annual return over the course of the investment period. See the following table for example:

	Annual Return	Dollar Gain (Loss)	Money Contributed (Distributed)	Portfolio Value
Initial Amount				$10,000.00
Year 1	12.0%	$1,200.00	$0.00	$11,200.00
Year 2	13.0%	$1,456.00	($1,000.00)	$11,656.00
Year 3	7.0%	$815.92	$1,500.00	$13,971.92
Year 4	15.0%	$2,095.79	$7,500.00	$23,567.71
Year 5	-9.0%	($2,121.09)	$0.00	$21,446.62
Annualized Return	7.6%			

Investment Mistakes 21

"Time-weighted return" is a misnomer because, as you may have noticed, the annualized return is not weighted at all! It is just the average return, without putting any additional weight on certain years. In the above example, the annualized return is:

(12.0% + 13.0% + 7.0% + 15.0% − 9.0%) ÷ 5 years = 7.6% per year

This number says very little about the wealth accrued to the client because it does not take into account the contributions to the fund and distributions to the investor. Most significantly, the investor contributed $7,500 right before she had the worst annual return of -9.0%.

The IRR ("money-weighted return"), in contrast, takes into consideration the decisions made to either contribute or distribute financial capital. See the same chart below, but with IRR calculated:

	Annual Return	Dollar Gain (Loss)	Money Contributed (Distributed)	Portfolio Value
Initial Amount				$10,000.00
Year 1	12.0%	$1,200.00	$0.00	$11,200.00
Year 2	13.0%	$1,456.00	($1,000.00)	$11,656.00
Year 3	7.0%	$815.92	$1,500.00	$13,971.92
Year 4	15.0%	$2,095.79	$7,500.00	$23,567.71
Year 5	-9.0%	($2,121.09)	$0.00	$21,446.62
IRR	4.18%			

The IRR is a percentage value which explains the way we got from the initial portfolio value to the current portfolio value, taking into consideration all the money taken out of and put into the portfolio along the way. **Since most people need to add and subtract cash from their invested assets over time, the IRR does a significantly better job of explaining changes in an investor's wealth than the annualized return does.** Notice that the IRR for the same portfolio is lower in this example because the IRR takes into consideration the fact that a large contribution was made to the fund right before a large downturn.

Most investment advisors are not interested in providing their clients with an IRR as a performance measurement. First, providing the IRR requires a log of all transactions into and out of a client's portfolio. Moreover, IRRs can often be less flattering to investment advisors' performance than annualized returns are. Despite the resistance to provide an IRR, individuals should insist that their financial advisors provide such a measure in order to get a clear idea of the progression of their wealth over time.

Risk-adjusted Performance Measures

IRR is not a perfect performance measure because it does not account for the riskiness of investments in computing the return accrued to the investor. **Much more important than the return to investors is the return per unit of risk. Just as it is unreasonable to assume that equities are always a better investment than government bonds, so too, it is unreasonable to judge investment managers based solely on their returns without considering the risks they take.**

There are a few standardized measures of *risk-adjusted return*,[2] but these, too, are imperfect performance indicators. Each one measures risk as the volatility of returns rather than the risk of permanently losing money. For wealthy individuals, who often have sufficient cash or incomes to weather short-term volatility, these measures fail to encapsulate the role of an investment manager or advisor.

A Reasoned Approach to Performance Evaluation

It is crucial that clients evaluate their investment professionals based on a combination of factors rather than any one single number. IRR and risk-adjusted performance measurements are useful because they measure some very important aspects of investment performance. However, among many other things, performance measurement should also be based on:

- Past instances of permanent losses.
- Duration of positive track record.
- Word-of-mouth references from current and former clients.
- Recommendations from trusted financial professionals.
- Whether the manager can articulate appropriate answers to probing questions.

In the end, IRR, risk-adjusted returns, and other performance factors should all be considered by clients looking to get a comprehensive understanding of a financial professional's performance. Clients should insist on the availability of all these important pieces of information so that they can make informed decisions.

The Bottom Line

Although wealthy families face considerable complexity in trying to approach their investments sensibly and creatively, implementing a few focused tips, like the ones discussed in this chapter, can make a great deal of difference over time.

The role of an investment consultant should be to help make his or her clients better investors by providing impartial advice and explaining where clients may be making costly mistakes. For their part, wealthy individuals and families who are not completely satisfied with their investment process should hold their investment professionals to a higher standard, wherever possible. As discussed in the next chapter, we believe that having an independent investment consultant is the best way for high-net-worth individuals and families to avoid their most common mistakes.

"No matter how great the talent or efforts, some things just take time. You can't produce a baby in one month by getting nine women pregnant."

- Warren Buffett

Chapter Two
Apples and Oranges
Product vs. Process

A few months before writing this chapter, a colleague of ours was attending a charity gala and started a conversation with the gentleman seated next to him. Before long, the two of them were discussing each other's jobs. Trying to wrap his head around what our colleague does, the gentleman asked our colleague:

> "Bottom line: If I entrusted you with $10 million today, what would you do with my money?"

Even though the gentleman wanted to cut to the heart of the matter, we get asked this question quite often and there is no simple answer. The process of answering the question of how one should invest his or her wealth cannot (and should not) be done in an elevator pitch. In short, the answer to the question is always:

> "It depends on you."

If this answer is unsatisfying, it is probably because the question implicitly mislabels how we believe investment advisory should be done. In fact, it insinuates an approach to investing that, as this chapter will discuss, we take issue with.

The question we feel much more comfortable answering is:

> *"If I came to you with $10 million, how would you help me become a sophisticated investor and make wiser investment decisions?"*

There is a big difference between the two questions and this difference forms the basis of this chapter. The question "how would you manage my money" is a bad conversation-starter because it implies a *product*-based way of approaching investment guidance. We believe that clients should be served in a fundamentally different way: with *process*-based investment guidance.

This chapter is divided into five sections. The first section discusses the "product-process distinction," which provides a framework to evaluate all goods and services. The second section explains how and why people are instinctively inclined towards products rather than processes, and some of the downfalls in this type of decision-making. In the third section, this chapter shows how product-based services have permeated the financial advisory business (to the detriment of clients) and some of the history leading up to our current state of affairs. The fourth section explains why this trend has occurred over time. In the last section, we explain the model of process-based financial advisory, the benefits of the model, and how clients can achieve such a relationship with their financial advisors. Ultimately, the point of this chapter is to help people know what to look for and, in the end, make better investment decisions.

1. Product vs. Process

A *product*-based service is one in which a professional has the end product in mind, and a ready-made entity to be sold, before knowing anything about the client. Most goods and services fall into this category. A grocery store, for example, offers a product-based service. Product-based services are provided to the customer with little input from the customer on what he or she is getting. The provider sells the same thing to different customers.

A *process*-based service, on the other hand, is a service for which the professional needs to know a lot about the client before offering guidance. Moreover, the person who receives the service[1] is, by definition, an active part of the end-result. A healthy relationship between a doctor (think G.P., not surgeon) and a patient is an example of a process-based service. A good doctor will be there every step of the way to help the patient get exactly what he or she needs to make the right decisions. That being said, the doctor cannot offer a ready-made entity to solve all the patient's problems. A doctor can provide expertise and tell patients how to preserve their health according to best practices. However, the patients will ultimately determine whether they take care of their own bodies. The unique circumstances of each patient will determine the prognoses. This is process-based service in a nutshell.

Unlike product-based services, the end-result for process-based services does not even exist until the service provider and the client develop it together. Indeed, there may not even be an "end-result" in the traditional sense because the process is ongoing, addressing the client's needs as they arise and change over time.

Process-based services tend to address long-standing issues rather than one-time fixes. For this reason, in addition to GPs, other process-based service providers include relationship counselors, personal trainers, life coaches and mentors. Going back to the question asked to our colleague at the charity gala, we can see why the question "If I gave you $10 million, what would you do with it?" pre-supposes that financial advisors are product-focused. **A process-focused financial advisor cannot** answer that question because he or she would not offer a quick fix to the problem. The advisor would instead take a step back and provide the client with a framework within which the two of them can *together* answer the question of how to meet the client's ultimate goals. Only then should the client rely on the advisor to implement their collective vision.

Summary of Product vs. Process Distinction for Financial Services

Product-Based Service	Process-Based Service
Unliateral Relationship Producer → Consumer	Collaborative Relationship Producer ←→ Consumer
Ready-made product offering. What the customer gets is largely predetermined.	Product development takes time and can only occur when the service provider learns about the client.
Sales Culture Goal: "Closing"	Fiduciary Culture Goal: Achieving goals of client
Compensation includes commissions, trailers, revenue sharing with third-parties, proprietary "in-house" products, etc. disclosed and undisclosed	Compensation comes only from the client. Eliminates conflict of interests.
Opaque. Client sees only the end result.	Transparent. Client sees product creation and is an integral part of developing the end results.

2. The Choice - Why People (Too Often) Choose Products over Process

Woody Allen once summed up people's eternal desire to buy products to solve life's problems.

> *"My father was fired. He was technologically unemployed. My father had worked for the same firm for 12 years. They fired him and replaced him with a tiny gadget that does everything my father does; only it does it much better. The depressing thing is, my mother ran out and bought one."*

The desire for products is so entrenched in our history that artifacts of advertising messages date back to 4,000 B.C.! Well before the printing press, the ancient Egyptians used papyrus to produce sales messages. Even when the vast majority of people were illiterate and lived in poverty, producers used "billboards" with images to advertise their product offerings. Today, mankind's propensity to be pitched to is arguably best exemplified by the staggering (and growing) infomercial industry, which enjoys an estimated $91 billion a year in sales.

Most people naturally follow the path of least resistance and have to work hard to quell that tendency. As human beings, if we could buy something at Walmart that would settle a family dispute, teach our children to do their homework and keep us following the diet that worked so well last year, we probably would. Unfortunately, when it comes to these types of issues, we live in a world where the path of least resistance yields, at best, mediocre results, and the latest technology cannot resolve life's most complex challenges. Issues pertaining to relationships, health and, yes, personal investing, require a process, not a product, because they need constant and consistent attention over a long period of time. As John F. Kennedy once brilliantly remarked, *"Mothers all want their sons to grow up to be president, but they don't want them to become politicians in the process.*"

Our tendency towards easy solutions is only exacerbated by the presence of marketing professionals determined to capitalize on our weaknesses. Given the tremendous resources spent on advertising (and the commensurate profits for people who work in the industry), companies certainly do not hesitate to bombard us with the idea that their product can solve our life's nagging issues. This type of advertising is perhaps no more problematic anywhere than in the wealth management industry, where clients are often sold products which are supposed to achieve their financial goals with no work required.

In and of itself, humanity's inclination towards buying products is not necessarily a problem. There are many products that address specific needs and have improved our ability to live the lives we want to live. The personal computer, for example, increased our working efficiency and ability to communicate across long distances for little cost. Kitchen appliances, clothing, furniture, food – these are all products that we value and are well served to buy in addressing certain needs.

The problems with product-orientation arise when we try to use products as the silver bullet for solving life's long-term and complicated problems – be they in parenting, healthy living, romantic relationships or financial success. These issues are specific to our personal situations and cannot be solved with products designed for public consumption. To grapple with such things, people need a process-based approach rather than a product-based one.

3. The Commoditization of Investment Advisory

Unfortunately, the vast majority of private wealth management is product-based, as clients are usually passive recipients of their investment strategies. As this section will discuss, there are serious problems that arise from financial services being product-based. Like health and relationships, investment success is particular to each person's needs and is part of a long-term issue which cannot be bought or relegated away.

The prevalence of products in the investment advisory industry is a result of what can be called "commoditization." Commoditization involves breaking down services to their simplest, lowest denominator and selling them like commodities. Once again, in and of itself, commoditization is healthy when it addresses specific needs in the market. Problems arise, however, when it involves taking a product or service which should never be commoditized, and making it so.

Historically, before the late 20th Century, the distinction between product and process in the investing industry was best exemplified by the difference between "brokers" and "advisors." Over time, however, commercial banks started buying brokerage houses and the industry changed dramatically. There was arguably nothing more significant and beneficial for the Canadian banks' shareholders in modern history than the acquisition of broker-dealers in the late 1980s.[2] Previous regulations prevented such activity[3] but as financial markets liberalized, bank mergers across North America brought brokerage houses into financial advisory and, in the process, invited the foxes into the hen-house.

Before the mergers, a broker's primary objective was to facilitate a transaction between two parties, making a profit ("spread") from each party. Brokers were pure product-people, offering a valuable platform through which many different customers could execute the same transaction efficiently and cost-effectively. Much like a sophisticated grocery store or a mall, brokers offered a location for exchange between buyers and sellers. Advisors, on the other hand, would work for only one party, typically on the "buy side" of the transaction, and, alongside their clients, select investments specific to their needs and wants. In doing so, advisors got paid only by their clients (rather than third parties) and helped them deal with sophisticated salespeople whose objectives were diametrically opposed to their own.

After financial deregulation brought commercial banks and brokerage houses under the same roof, the barrier between brokers and advisors became muddled in the wealth management industry. These developments had a terrible effect on the alignment of interests between wealth management professionals and their clients.

The problems now go well beyond the brokerage house and affect private client groups. So-called "advisors" often get a significant proportion of their income from commissions, trailers and revenue sharing agreements with third parties, creating incentives which directly conflict with client interests. Proprietary "in-house" investment products have a similar effect on interests-misalignment because advisor bonuses are based on the product being sold rather than achieving the goals of the person buying it.

The difference between product-based services and process-based services can also be summed up in what Maria Elena Lagomasino, CEO of Genspring Family Offices[4], refers to as the difference between "sales culture" and "fiduciary culture." The key is the mindset of the professional: is the professional firmly in the client's corner or is there some trade-off for the professional between personal interests and client interests?

The mixing of sales culture and fiduciary culture results in a Frankenstein of investment advisory in which clients are sold products when they think they are getting impartial advice.

If investing were a one-time or short-term need, rather than an ongoing process, and did not need to be specific to each person's individual situation, then the prevalence of products would not matter. Problems with product-based investment advisory arise because investing is a long process that, much like personal health and relationships, cannot be solved by quick-fixes.

In investment consulting, the experience and end-result from the client's perspective are much more positive in a process-based system. In process-based financial advisory, there is a better understanding and sense of comfort on the part of the client, a better customization and assurance that the client's personal needs are taken care of and a better chance that the professional is kept honest and determined to serve the client well. For those financial service providers who focus primarily on products, their clients are less informed, more stressed, more anxious, and ultimately end up with investments which are unlikely to serve their purposes.

Sources of Portfolio Underperformance

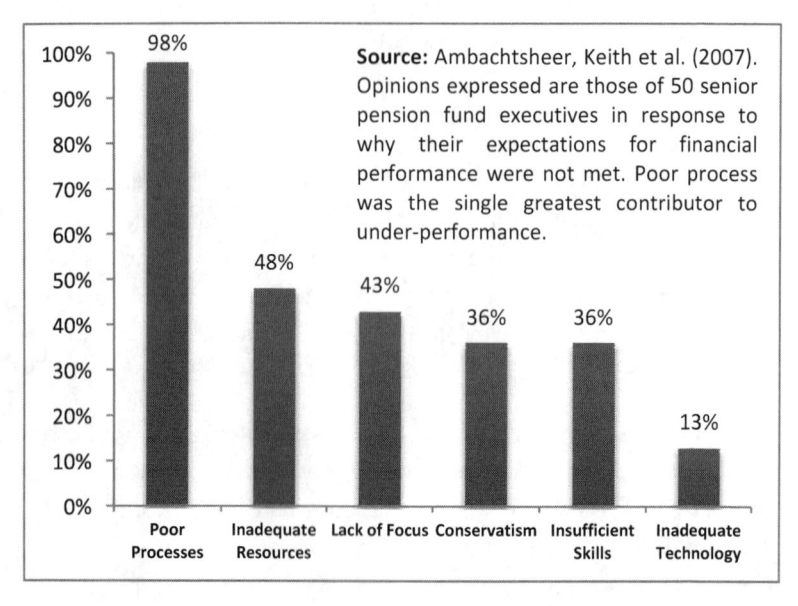

Category	Percentage
Poor Processes	98%
Inadequate Resources	48%
Lack of Focus	43%
Conservatism	36%
Insufficient Skills	36%
Inadequate Technology	13%

Source: Ambachtsheer, Keith et al. (2007). Opinions expressed are those of 50 senior pension fund executives in response to why their expectations for financial performance were not met. Poor process was the single greatest contributor to under-performance.

4. Why Products Dominate the Investment Advisory Industry:

There are several reasons investment services for high-net-worth individuals and families are so commoditized. First, commodities – like fruit, oil and gold – are simple to define and understand. As a result, marketing teams tend to love commoditization. They generally prefer to simplify their services rather than complicate the explanation of what their company does.

Although we believe that simplification is important, we also believe that simplification should not come at the expense of transparency, customization and providing a multifaceted service. Investment advisory, which should be tailored to the client, should not be commoditized and turned into a product-based service.

The problem with offering a process-based service, from a marketing perspective, is that the service is not tangible unless someone is already involved in it. There is no final product to show prospective clients – to "wow" them with or to convince them of its usefulness. **In an industry like finance, in which there is asymmetrical information between clients and professionals[5], commoditization can lead people to buy things they do not need or overpay for those they do.**

Second, many investment professionals often do not like process-based services because process-based services are not as scalable and profitable as product-based services are. They simply take too much time and effort. Investing touches on all aspects of a person's life: not only their age and family situation, but also their personal aspirations and preferences. In a process-based service, flushing out all the requisite pieces of personal information is a key aspect of the service. Often, people do not even know what their own preferences are, so it is the responsibility of the professional to ask probing questions and illicit the client's own sense of direction. The client should learn something about himself or herself in the investment process. Due to the product-based nature of most investment services, however, most people would never consider their experiences with financial service providers to be ones of personal growth, self-exploration and education.

Another reason investment services (for high-net-worth clients and others) are so commoditized is that many professionals earn a significant proportion of their income from third parties. Investment advisors may not get paid for delivery of advice without the sale of a financial product. For example, an "advisor" may earn the majority of his or her income based on how many trades a client makes or how much money the client puts in their brokerage account. This service provider would not earn anything for instructing the client to just "sit tight," even though such advice can be incredibly valuable at times. Sometimes, sitting on more cash is healthy. Although this pay scheme does not mean that the services rendered are always perverse, it is naive to think that such policies do not negatively affect the industry.

As long as service providers are given an economic incentive to choose certain products over others (or any products at all), clients will, by and large, find themselves with a skewed offering. Trailers and commissions are the bane of investment advisory. That is why we believe in (and actually practice) forwarding the savings of all commissions and trailers to clients, deducting them against fees.[6]

Yet another reason the industry is so commoditized is that an increasing amount of investment services are provided by large banks that have a strong incentive to provide product-focused services. Large banks, many of which bought-out their high-net-worth advisory practices, are understandably focused on their return on investment and the price of their stock. Unfortunately, the returns from providing product-based services are, by nature, much higher than those from providing process-based services. For example, changing the legal standard of responsibility from that of a sales-type firm to a fiduciary could cost a firm like Morgan Stanley an estimated 6%-7% percent of their annual earnings.[7]

Despite efforts to maintain a separation between bank departments, the cohabitation of corporate finance, brokerage and advisement under the same roof often leads to serious agency issues. The "in-house" products of these institutions are often promoted without regard for what is truly best for the client. **In general, clients are best serviced when fiduciary culture and sales culture are *completely* segregated and when their advisory needs are provided by a company that does not also work in the sales industry.**

5. Avoiding the Pitfalls - How to Bring Process to Your Investing

The most sophisticated investors — whether they are pension funds, endowments, foundations or family offices — typically approach their investing in a process-focused way. They typically hire a team of investment professionals whose sole purpose is to represent their interests. The head of the investment team is usually called a Chief Investment Officer (CIO). At Prime Quadrant, we have worked very hard to provide the CIO function to individuals and families, even in the $5M-$30M investable-asset range, at a fraction of the cost of hiring a team of "in-house" investment professionals.[8]

The image of a CIO cannot be painted with broad strokes because his or her role will depend on the needs of each individual client. That being said, there are some unique attributes of a CIO that are easily distinguishable from those of product-focused service providers. A CIO's compensation, rather than being based on commissions and revenue sharing, is based on a flat-fee retainer. His or her financial incentive is to maintain a long-term, trusted relationship with clients. The amount of time that CIOs take to learn about a client is extensive, and recouping compensation for that time spent can only be done when the client decides to retain the services over the long-term.

A CIO is on the payroll of the person to whom he or she owes fiduciary duty and does not earn third-party compensation. Third-parties, such as financial product salespeople, fund-managers and other "sell side" investment professionals are selected for the client based purely on their propensity to serve the client well.

We believe that high-net-worth individuals and families could learn a lot from professional golf players. The most dominant golfers in history have all had coaches. Greats like Jack Nicklaus, Tiger Woods and Gary Player, no matter how naturally talented, sought out guidance from an objective third party in an effort to improve their crafts. Although the coaches may not be as talented as the players are, they offer tremendous value by being knowledgeable, impartial and trustworthy. The CIO provides the same value in investing, although usually with the additional benefit of being accomplished in the field.

The relationship between a CIO and client is different than the typical relationship between clients and money managers. **If the advisor is the Chief Investment Officer (CIO), the client is the Chief Executive Officer (CEO). After a CIO offers a professional opinion,** *the client makes the ultimate decision.* **Although this relationship requires additional work from the client, the level of transparency is incomparably better than that which most clients get in their investment management.**

The benchmark for success of a CIO is also different. At the end of the day, there should only be one benchmark: the needs, goals and aspirations of the client. For this reason, a CIO does not hold himself or herself to a standard dictated by the broader market (i.e. the S&P 500 or any other index) but rather to the standard dictated by the client. These standards are determined in the course of a many hours of conversation between the CIO and the client at the beginning of the relationship and thereafter. The choice of benchmark strongly influences investment decisions and cannot be relegated to events that occur beyond the personal requirements of each client.

Summarizing the Role of a CIO:

- Works with the client over many hours of conversation to determine the client's risk tolerance

and return needs. Compiles this information, using plain language, in the investment policy statement.
- Provides a flow of new investment opportunities which align with the specific needs of the client.
- Acts as the client's advocate to salespeople and fund managers. A CIO has more expertise in the industry and can therefore be an expert "shopper" of opportunities.
- Acts as a sounding board for ideas, providing constructive feedback. A CIO is not only a source of investment ideas but also, just as importantly, an evaluator of others' investment ideas.
- Helps the client focus on the big picture and eliminate rash decision-making. Makes sure the client keeps calm and carries on, when appropriate.
- Collaborates with the client's various service providers to tie together the investment picture. Works with lawyers, accountants, estate planners, and charities, among others.
- Screens bad ideas to make efficient use of the client's time.
- Oversees the execution of investment decisions, ensuring the client's interests are taken care of.

With the exception of Prime Quadrant and one or two peers, the outsourced CIO role for high-net-worth families is largely absent in Canada. However, it is well developed and common in the European and U.S. markets. As more clients become informed about the perils of product-focused investment services, we expect to see the proliferation of process-focused investment consulting.

The Bottom Line

There is an important distinction between process-based investment services and product-based investment services. Although the industry, in general, has blurred the lines over time, clients should never allow the two types of services to be conflated. Knowing whether one is receiving the former or the latter can save a tremendous amount of frustration and prevent many sleepless nights. Whereas product-based investment services can be a "black box" for investors and are wrought with potential conflicts of interest, process-based investment services are transparent and result in the investor playing an active role in the relationship.

We do not mean to imply that product-based investment services have no place in the world. Their scalability and availability to the general public make them very useful in the retail market. That being said, far too many (if not most) investors require a process-based investment service and only get products in its place. This is particularly true for high-net-worth individuals and families. For any Permitted Clients,[9] it is worthwhile spending the time and energy required to develop a portfolio customized to suit their particular wants and needs. They would be well served to recognize the conflicts that arise from product-based services for so-called investment "advisory" and insist on partaking in more process-oriented investing.

As we mentioned earlier, the point of this chapter is to help you know what to look for when evaluating investment services and, in the end, to make better investment decisions. There is a good deal of information in this chapter, but the take-away is brief: when it comes to managing one's own wealth, focusing on the process rather than the products can make all the difference. As we often say, take care of the process and the products will take care of themselves.

"I'd be a bum on the street with a tin cup if the markets were efficient."

- Warren Buffett

Chapter Three
Inefficient Markets
The Secrets of Outperformance

On Monday, October 19th, 1989, financial markets went through a catastrophe. In one single day, many of the world's major indexes lost more than one-fifth of their market value. The Dow Jones Index, for example, went down 22.61% over a 24-hour period.

What explains this precipitous decline? What explains the fact that the losses were largely eliminated as the market rebounded over the next two days? Most importantly: what would have been the best approach to navigating such daunting circumstances?

The answers to these questions center on the idea of market efficiency. Market efficiency refers to *the ability of financial markets to quickly and correctly price investments*. Although many academics and professionals believe that financial markets are efficient, the events of October 19th (often referred to as "Black Monday") are certainly a thorn in the side of efficient market believers. If financial markets were correctly pricing investments on Monday, then what made the markets change their minds on Tuesday and Wednesday? The truth is that financial markets are often not efficient, as this chapter will discuss.

There are important implications about market inefficiency which affect all investors, and we will try to shed some light on the whole issue.

The first part of this chapter explains what an efficient market is. The second part discusses why the topic of efficient markets should matter to everyone and not just to academics and professionals. The third part covers risk-adjusted returns. The fourth part will explain why we reject the theory of efficient markets. Finally, the fifth part will outline four lessons for high-net-worth individuals and families given what is discussed in this chapter.

1. Efficient Markets

If a market is efficient, the prices of investments adapt very quickly and accurately to new information. In fact, prices change so quickly in such a market that it is impossible for investors to make a profit by knowing a lot about an investment. As a result, people investing their money in an "efficient" market are surprisingly restricted in the way that they can earn more money. **In an efficient market, the only way a person can make more money is if he or she takes on more risk.**

Say, for example, that I know a lot about investing in a specific sector. Let's even say that it is an obscure sector, like the manufacturing of dolls. After researching the bustling doll sector, I find out about a doll manufacturing plant in Omaha, which has publically announced a change in its manufacturing technique.

I realize, with my expertise, that this manufacturing change will increase the value of the company by four times. Last week, before the announcement, the company's stock was trading at $5.00 per share. When I rush to place a buy order right after the announcement, however, the stock price has already risen to

$20.00 per share and I cannot make my abnormally high profit. The price already reflects the new value of the company because it adapted instantly and accurately.

In an efficient market, this will always happen because information about each investment is spread so broadly across the market that anything one investor knows, everyone knows.

In a way, the market is considered to be "smart" and "fast" – at least smarter and faster than any single investor or group of investors. In such a market, the only way to make more money investing is to do something riskier which warrants higher compensation.

When markets are inefficient, on the other hand, investors can take advantage of the fact that prices are sometimes "wrong," meaning that the prices do not reflect the intrinsic value of assets. When this is the case, intelligent, informed, diligent and objective investors are "smarter" than the market and can earn higher risk-adjusted profits with their expertise.

In an efficient market, investment skill – based on intelligence, diligence, objectivity – is useless and a person can only get a higher return if they take on more risk. In an inefficient market, however, people can benefit from their expertise and earn more money without taking on additional risk.

2. Why is this Important?

Everyone who invests their money, from the casual e*trader to the investment banker, is faced with the choice of whether to be in the "inefficient market camp" or the "efficient market camp." Is it smart to invest with active managers (mutual funds, hedge funds, brokers) who take a fee in exchange for their expertise in investing clients' money? Or is it more prudent to invest only in passive portfolios (ETFs and indexes) because any supposed expertise has no value in investing? Is it necessary to make risky decisions if one wants to make more money? These are questions that all people face.

3. Risk-Adjusted Returns

We all want to earn money with our investments but very few of us want to increase our chance of losing money in the process. For this reason, earning higher risk-adjusted returns is the goal of every intelligent investor. Higher risk-adjusted returns occur when people get higher returns without taking on more risk or the same returns while taking less risk. They occur when investors get more 'bang for their buck.'

One way to earn higher risk-adjusted returns is by having the proper asset allocation and diversifying. (While this chapter does not discuss asset allocation, for more about that topic please refer to Chapters Five and Six). **If markets are efficient, implementing a proper asset allocation and diversifying is the only way to earn higher risk-adjusted returns.**

The other way to earn higher risk-adjusted returns, which is only possible when markets are inefficient, is by consistently picking investments which can be bought for less than their intrinsic value. Such investments have upsides that are disproportionately high compared to their downsides. The ability to find these investments is often called "security selection" and describes what most people picture when they think of investment skill.

Security selection involves a deep understanding of individual investments and the nature of financial markets.

Earning higher risk-adjusted returns with superior security selection is not possible in an efficient market because investing knowledge is considered to be so well diffused across the market that it is useless. In contrast, inefficient markets allow investors to find mispriced assets and then wait for the market to "correct," earning higher profits in the process.[1]

Thankfully, investment skill is, in fact, useful because markets are not always efficient, as the next section discusses.

4. Rejecting Efficient Markets

> *"Be Fearful When Others Are Greedy and Greedy When Others Are Fearful."*
>
> *- Howard Marks*

There are many reasons to reject the notion that all markets are efficient. Three of these reasons are discussed in this chapter. They can be divided into the Keynesian Rationale, the Unique Market Rationale, and the Historical Rationale.

The Keynesian: Animal Spirits

In his seminal book, *The General Theory of Employment, Interest and Money* (1936), Economist John Maynard Keyes used the term "animal spirits" to describe the market sentiment which influences the economy. He wrote about how optimistic and pessimistic expectations influence the ebbs and flows of economic growth.

When people are optimistic overall, investment returns increase because people are willing to be a little looser with their money. When people are pessimistic overall, investment returns decrease because people are more tight-fisted, worrying that they may need to save money for tough times ahead.

Howard Marks, investing guru and chairman of Oaktree Capital Management, also wrote about the balance in financial markets between fear and greed. When investors are motivated predominantly by fear, prices are often depressed because people's concerns lead them to sell at any cost and avoid purchasing. When investors are motivated by greed, prices are often inflated because people lose sight of frugality in light of the prospect to strike it rich.

Whether it is optimism, pessimism, greed or fear, emotions affect the way that people invest. These emotions skew prices one way or the other, leaving room for more tempered people to invest according to the right information and to earn higher risk-adjusted returns over time.

Short-term, relative performance mentalities create a herding phenomenon, which causes money managers to buy and sell securities at approximately the same time.[2] This process invariably leads to market prices far above or far below their intrinsic value because supply and demand changes become exaggerated. Jeremy Grantham, Chief Investment Officer of GMO, a Boston-based asset management firm, once measured the variability in GDP growth, intrinsic value, and market prices to test the extent to which prices deviate from market fundamentals.[3] Grantham found that two-thirds of the time, GDP and intrinsic value growth varied within only 1% of their long-term trends. This finding is explained by the fact that GDP and the intrinsic value of companies do not change drastically over short time-periods. However, Grantham also found that market prices varied within 19% of their long-term trends!

Whereas GDP growth and intrinsic value are "sticky" and diverge very little from their long-term trends, market prices can vary wildly because they are dependent on the mentality of the people buying and selling shares. According to Grantham, herding is by far the largest factor that explains the wild divergences of market prices relative to GDP growth and intrinsic values.

Animal spirits cause the market to systematically misprice investments, which means that more objective, informed and diligent investors can consistently exploit mispricing.

The Unique Market: "Not All Markets Are Created Equal"

In addition to the fact that the overall market can be dominated by market sentiment, certain sectors are particularly prone to inefficiency. There are several reasons why one financial market may be more inefficient than another. Two of these reasons are: (a) society has, for some reason, developed a bias against it and (b) it is more complicated to understand.

For example, financial analysts tend to pay particular attention to the stocks of large companies. This trend is partially a by-product of the way the investment banking industry works, but is also due to the stature that "large-cap" stocks hold in society. People want to know how Apple (AAPL) is doing, and, every day, thousands of intelligent people pour over its financial statements trying to figure out where the company is headed. Trying to get an edge over the competition for these kinds of investments is exceptionally difficult, if not impossible, in normal markets. There are very few glaring inefficiencies for the stocks of these types of companies unless animal spirits are taking hold of the economy as a whole.

In the process, other investments are monitored by far fewer people. "Small-cap" stocks, for example, can often slip through the cracks of large institutions' financial analysts and go unmonitored. Many large institutions are required to move so much capital when they invest that they are restricted to companies of a certain size. Their restrictions open up opportunities for investors with more nimble capital, who are able to invest in all companies, large and small.

High-yield bonds is another sector which is notorious for mispricing. **Any investment which, for some unfounded reason, has a stigma against it leaves room for objective, informed and diligent investors to earn higher returns without more risk.**

There are also investments which are stigmatized because they are too complicated for generalist investors. Some sectors require inter-disciplinary approaches, such as investing in companies on the brink of bankruptcy (called "distressed" investing). This strategy requires interplay between finance professionals and legal professionals. Naturally, there are significantly fewer investors in these more complex sectors. **Of course, investors must be more careful when dealing with these types of investments, but specialists in a generalist investment field often earn higher risk-adjusted returns for themselves and for their clients.**

The Historical: The Superinvestors of Graham and Doddsville

Anyone would love to have invested with Warren Buffett when he first started investing in Berkshire Hathaway. Buffett's investors received an absurdly high 20.2% compounded return from 1965 to 2010. This return can be contrasted to the very respectable 9.4% compounded return for the S&P 500 over the same period. To put Buffett's accomplishment into perspective: if you were to have invested $100,000 with Buffett in 1965, by the end of 2010 you would have earned almost $400 million, compared to just over $5.5 million investing in the S&P 500.[4]

Buffett's staggering success begs a question. According to efficient market believers, investors cannot regularly earn higher risk-adjusted returns based on skill. How do efficient market proponents explain Warren Buffett's success? In short: luck.

If we could analyze other investors with similar skills as Buffett's, we might get a better idea of how much luck was involved in his success. If all of these investors turned out to achieve similar returns over long periods of time, it would indicate that something about Buffett's investing skill or knowledge was the source of his returns, and not dumb luck.

Despite Buffett's uniqueness, there are several investors who shared the same investment philosophy and started investing around the same time as he did. These investors were, like Buffett, the intellectual followers of Benjamin Graham and David Dodd. Graham and Dodd were the developers of the value investing philosophy and professors at Columbia University.

If investment returns were to be abnormally high across all of Graham and Dodd's disciples, then it would not be reasonable to view Warren Buffett's success as just lucky. Instead, it would make sense to say that something about these investors' shared process leads to investing success.

Buffett himself provided the evidence for this thought experiment in his paper "The Superinvestors of Graham and Doddsville". In the paper, Buffett analyzed the investment returns of Graham and Dodd's followers to see if they beat the market indexes over long periods of time. This experiment is not merely a case of picking the few investors that did well. For example, the first four investors on the following list were the only four employees at the Graham-Newman Corporation, who worked for Benjamin Graham from 1954 to 1956 before each started their own funds. Additionally, each manager invested in different securities and achieved his success in a different way.

Superinvestor	Annual Compound Rate	Equivalent Market Performance	Time-span (annual compound rate)
Walter J. Schloss (W.J.S. Limited Partners and WJS Partnership)	16.1% and 21.3% respectively	8.4% (S&P 500)	28 and one-quarter years
Tom Knapp (TBK Overall and Limited Partners)	16.0% and 20.0% respectively	7.0% (Dow)	15 and three-quarters years
Warren Buffett (Buffett Partnership and Limited Partnership)	23.8% and 29.5% respectively	7.4% (Dow)	13 years
William J. Ruane (Sequoia Fund)	17.2%	10.0% (S&P 500)	13 and three-quarters years
Charles Munger (Limited Partners and Overall Partnership)	13.7% and 19.8% respectively	5.0% (Dow)	14 years
Rick Guerin (Pacific Limited Partnership and Overall Partnership)	23.6% and 32.9% respectively	7.8% (S&P 500)	19 years
Stan Perlmeter (Limited Partners and Overall Partnership)	19.0% and 23.0% respectively	7.0% (Dow)	20 years

These statistics often bring up a good question: if it is so obvious that value investing can lead to higher risk-adjusted returns, why doesn't everybody just adopt the process?

This question can be compared to asking why everybody does not eat well and exercise every day. The truth is that value investing, although simple, is far from easy. It requires diligence, intelligence, good judgment, and tremendous amounts of patience and self-control – much like staying healthy does. Investors need to use deep analysis, buy securities with conviction and then withstand what can be frightening amounts of volatility. Both require knowledge and patience.

5. Four Investing Lessons for High-Net-Worth Families and Individuals

There are many lessons to be learned about investing that high-net-worth families and individuals can gather from this chapter.

To summarize the discussion so far, financial markets are certainly not always efficient. The market often misprices investments for a long enough period to allow intelligent, informed, diligent and objective investors to earn higher investment returns without taking on more risk. The reasons markets are not efficient have to do with the pervasiveness of emotions in financial markets and the complexities of investing in specific markets. The fact that value investors, in the tradition of Ben Graham and David Dodd, have been able to achieve such high returns over long periods of time shows that investors can benefit from these inefficiencies.

The takeaways from all this information are surprisingly helpful, specifically for high-net-worth families and individuals. The main ones are:

1. First and foremost, it is important to understand that markets can behave irrationally for very long periods of time – even years – so it is necessary and warranted to stay calm and keep a level head. Understanding exactly what you are invested in is the first and most important step in attaining this mindset. Your investments may be underpriced for nauseating amounts of time but, if the fundamentals are sound, patience will serve you better than any amount of genius will.

As Warren Buffett has said, "In the investing business, if you have an IQ of 150, sell 30 points to someone else. You do not need to be a genius. You need to have emotional stability, inner peace and be able to think for yourself."

Never sell an investment just because it declines in value. In fact, if markets go through an irrational decline, and you are still confident in the fundamentals of the investment, the best decision is to buy more after a drop in prices and then wait for the market to make sense again.

2. A related lesson is to embrace a long-term investment horizon if you have the means of doing so. Endowments, pension funds and high-net-worth families and individuals fall into this category because they usually have enough money to meet their short-term spending needs and obligations.

Investments that require long-term commitments often come with additional compensation for investors because of their restrictions on liquidity. If liquidity is less of an issue for you, consider longer-term investments which have the time to capitalize on short-term market inefficiencies and often come with more favourable terms for investors.

3. People who have the propensity to invest in alternative assets would be well served to do so.

Alternative investments – which include hedge funds, private equity, real estate and distressed investing, among others

– often focus on the less efficient markets discussed in Part 3 of this chapter. These investments require additional expertise to navigate but can provide the opportunity for higher returns with equal or less risk. They are predominantly used by endowments, pension funds, large institutions and high-net-worth investors because they come with greater complexity and additional fees and restrictions.

Alternative investments also tend to have longer-term investment horizons, which is important for the reasons described above.

4. If one is investing with an active manager, he or she should invest with an accomplished and experienced value investor.

Place a very high priority on finding a value-oriented investment manager who has achieved high returns over many years and does not have a history of permanently losing clients' money. An investment manager who follows a value investing philosophy and is diligent, informed, intelligent and objective is a good person to align one's investing with.

The Bottom Line

The overwhelming evidence suggests that markets are not efficient and investors can, in fact, earn higher returns on investments without taking on more risk. This information is not only useful for academics and professionals. Anyone who invests his or her money can benefit from market inefficiencies if they act strategically with this knowledge in mind. If done correctly, investing with a trusted professional can be worthwhile because skillful investors can earn higher returns with the same or less risk. If one does not possess the necessary skills, he or she can still benefit from market inefficiencies by aligning interests with someone who is.

This option is particularly useful for high-net-worth families and individuals because they have the propensity to use the services of informed, diligent, intelligent and objective investors as well as the financial flexibility to withstand short-term volatility. In addition to opening up the possibility of higher risk-adjusted returns, the knowledge that markets are sometimes inefficient also allows people to stave off panicking and even benefit when the markets go through tumultuous periods, as they did on Black Monday, October 19th, 1989.

"When any guy offers you a chance to earn lots of money without risk, don't listen to the rest of his sentence."

- Charles (Charlie) Munger

Chapter Four

Risky Business

Capitalizing on Uncertainty

When we first meet with clients, the first thing they say is: "I don't want to take a lot of risk." When we first meet with investment managers, they invariably claim: "What really differentiates us from our competitors is our risk management system." When we first meet peers in our industry, they always state: "We help our clients maximize returns while minimizing risk."

It seems that the word "risk" is on everyone's mind – but do all these people mean the same thing? Let's dig a bit deeper and try to determine some possible interpretations:

WHAT CLIENTS SAY: **"I don't want to take a lot of risk."**

WHAT CLIENTS MIGHT MEAN:
- I don't want to face another 2008 scenario where my portfolio is down 40%. My stomach won't be able to handle huge up-and-down swings.
- I don't want any financial uncertainty over the next five years.
- I don't want to lose money.

WHAT MANAGERS SAY: "What really differentiates us from our competitors is our risk management system."

WHAT MANAGERS MIGHT MEAN:
- Our performance will exhibit less volatility.
- We avoid permanently losing capital and will earn better returns than our peers.
- We have PhDs and engineers that program complex algorithms to reduce and control the risk in our portfolio.

WHAT ADVISORS SAY: "We help our clients maximize returns while minimizing risk."

WHAT ADVISORS MIGHT MEAN:
- We buy what large and sophisticated institutions buy. They have strict investment criteria, so it must be good.
- We recommend investments that have had a nice run. That way, we know it's a good time to get in.
- We recommend investments that have extremely solid fundamentals so that you can't go wrong investing in them.

Clearly, the word "risk" can mean very different things to different people. This discrepancy is stark because the marketplace is made up of many different participants: individual investors, pension plans, endowments, hedge funds, sovereign wealth funds and mutual funds, to name a few. Each participant has their own agenda, their own objectives and constraints. A portfolio manager working at a large mutual fund may view the riskiness of a less-recognized company entirely different than a portfolio manager working at a hedge fund. Coca Cola stock, for example, could be considered to have little risk, or extreme risk, depending on the investor who buys it.

    This chapter discusses the way we view risk and debunks much of the common lore about how investors should approach it. The first part of this chapter provides a brief word on risk as it relates to volatility. The second part shares nine ideas about risk. The third part discusses how one can go about measuring risk and some of the shortfalls of the most commonly used measurements. The fourth part explains how investors can use the rest of the information in this chapter to take advantage of risk and help achieve their financial goals.

Part I: A Word on Risk and Volatility

The predominant belief among investment professionals and academics is that risk is measured by the volatility of the underlying asset. Simply put, volatility is a measure of how drastically the price has moved up and down over time. It is assumed that the more volatile an asset's short-term price has been in the past, the more risky it is.

Many academics and investment professionals want a single statistic that measures risk. They want this measure to be quantifiable, easy, and convenient. Volatility is the ideal candidate, while other definitions of risk simply are not. It is easy to calculate historical volatility. Academics and professionals measuring risk in this way are able to extrapolate and model future "risk," so that they can construct mathematical models and allocate investments accordingly.

In reality, risk is not so easily quantifiable, easy or convenient: It is multifaceted. There are many, more significant, types of risk that affect market participants. With this idea in mind, this chapter provides nine thoughts on risk that investors should be mindful of.

Part II: Nine Ideas on Risk
1. Career Risk

For the vast majority of investment managers - whether they are managing money for a mutual fund, pension plan, or a high-net-worth family - their number one priority is, unfortunately, to keep their jobs. At the same time, for many of these professionals, performance is evaluated against several benchmarks on a monthly, quarterly, and annual basis (some managers are actually evaluated on an hourly basis!). If they want to keep their jobs, they must never underperform any of the benchmarks at any short-term interval. And to avoid underperformance, they must rarely, if ever, stray from the status quo.

"Career risk" is the risk that the security of the investment manager's job takes precedence over the security of the client's money in the investment decision making process.

Paying strict attention to what other investors are doing and "going with the flow" at best ensures an acceptable mediocrity. While implementing unconventional ideas often appears imprudent, it is also the basis for long-term investment success.

While career risk is seldom discussed, it is very important to consider. Investors must understand the implications of the fact that most money managers' top priority is to keep their well-paying jobs. This reality is unfortunate because many of the best investment ideas are unpopular and criticized when first initiated, and few managers have the resilience to withstand the pressure.

Career risk can be minimized in certain ways, many of which were discussed in Chapter Two. Investors should pay attention to the fee structure and incentives that their financial advisors have. It is important for investors to maintain a long-term outlook and compensate their financial advisors accordingly.

2. Falling Short of One's Goals

Different investors have different needs. As such, one of the first things we do with a client (and recommend for everyone to follow suit) is create their very own cash flow statement. Their sources of income, ordinary/one-time expenses, taxes and inflation are taken into account to come up with the minimum return required to live the lifestyle they choose.

An individual who could live extremely comfortably earning 3% a year should have no urgency (and perhaps no reason to take on the additional risk) of earning 6% a year. On the other hand, a pension fund that has to achieve an 8% return a year would find itself in serious trouble if returns averaged 6% over an extended period of time. A "risk-free" investment earning 5% a year would be riskless for the individual but very risky for the pension plan.

Risk is not an abstract concept – it should be rooted in the practical needs of the individual, family or institution investing. Creating an investment policy statement, as we discussed in Chapter Two, helps investors understand their required return based on the only metric that matters: themselves. Adherence to a rigorous investment process is the best way to protect against the risk of falling short of one's goals.

3. Leverage

The most common form of leverage is borrowing capital in hopes of increasing the investor's expected return. For example:

consider a corporate bond that pays a coupon of 6% a year. An investor with $100 would receive six dollars per year for a return of 6%. What if the investor deemed the 6% return inadequate? One thing she could do is borrow $400, paying 5% interest on it, and invest this capital into the same bond. She would now have $500 to invest instead of $100.

This investor would generate $30 (6% on the $500) in coupon income and need to repay $20 in interest costs (5% interest on the $400 she borrowed) leaving her with $10 profit ($30 minus $20) on $100 of equity capital. Excellent! She just transformed the inadequate 6% return into a beautiful 10% return.

Investors seem to forget (or choose to ignore) the other side of the story – leverage can magnify losses as well as the gains. Leverage is the ultimate double-edged sword. Borrowing capital cannot change the probability of an investment decision being right or wrong. All it does is magnify the end-result, while increasing the risk profile of a portfolio. Leverage cannot make a bad investment good, but it can make a good investment bad. In the example above, if the bond decreases significantly in price or, worse, defaults, the investor now owes more money to lenders than she has.

Take the case of Long-Term Capital Management (LTCM). LTCM was a hedge fund that employed, relative to its size, as many Nobel Prize Laureates and PhDs as any organization in the world, including, at the time, Microsoft and IBM. The hedge fund engaged in various complex trading strategies to take advantage of minute discrepancies between virtually identical fixed income assets, particularly in the U.S., Japanese, and European government bond markets. Because the discrepancies were so small, LTCM leveraged their capital 25 to 1 (they had equity of $4.72 billion and had borrowed approximately $125 billion). Leverage of 25 to 1 implies that a 4% decline in the value of the fund would wipe out 100% of the equity. The story sequence is one of the oldest in the books:

1. LTCM took on excessive leverage to inflate inadequate unleveraged returns.

2. One day, something "out of the ordinary" happened, which adversely affected their investments (out of the ordinary events seem to happen on a regular basis).

3. The lenders, afraid that the collateral behind the loans would become worth less than the loans themselves, demanded their money back.

4. In order to repay the loans, LTCM was forced to sell investments.

5. Because other leveraged investors were also trying to sell the same investments at the same time, excess supply in the market depressed prices even further.

6. The other investments in LTCM's portfolio had to be marked down to levels that made its liabilities far exceed its assets. As a result, the fund became insolvent and went bankrupt.

For the first couple of years, LTCM produced 40%+ returns, until a few events wreaked havoc in the markets that LTCM was trading in. This led to large back-to-back monthly losses, margin calls from their various lenders, liquidation of a number of their positions at highly unfavorable prices, equity capital declining from $4.72 billion to under $400 million, and, finally, a bailout from Wall Street and other banks to avoid a financial meltdown. It should be no surprise that highly leveraged positions are the cause of most fund, company, and/or country collapses.

Recall the "inadequate" bond yielding 6%. One reason why an investor may feel this return is inadequate is because the bond is fairly overvalued. What happens when other investors come to this same realization? In order for the bond to become more attractive, its price must fall. Unfortunately, the investor now has five times as much of an asset that is producing an inadequate return and is in store for a price decline.

It is, therefore, incumbent on the investor to understand how much leverage a manager has undertaken, how much leverage their mandate allows, how much leverage is appropriate, and why.

4. Redemptions

The following quotation from a Torontonian investment manager perfectly expresses how important it is to co-invest with investors who will not redeem in times of crisis:

> "Every effort has been made to ensure we have the strongest capital base in the business. This investor base serves us well, so when markets sell off we are looking around at the great deals in the market and not wasting time and resources wondering where we will get money to fund redemptions."
>
> Warren Irwin, Q2 2012 Investor Letter, Rosseau Asset Management

Mass redemptions occur when markets are spiraling downward and investors are panicking. If cash levels are not sufficient to satisfy redemptions, the manager will be forced to sell investments immediately (likely at distressed prices). This forced selling puts further downward pressure on market prices and we find ourselves in a vicious cycle. Several times during the crash of 2008, the market dropped sharply during the final trading hour. This may be explained by the fact that mutual fund managers receive a summary of redemptions each afternoon and have to sell quickly to meet the redemptions by the following morning. It was not unusual for mutual funds to receive redemptions in excess of $5 billion a day! Unfortunately, in an ironic twist to the mass-redemption narratives, the costs of redemptions are ultimately borne by the investors who stick around.

It is important to pay attention to how a fund is structured. For example, Hedge Fund ABC and Hedge Fund XYZ both invest in the same small-cap stocks. Investors in ABC are unable to redeem for three years (closed-end structure) while investors in XYZ may redeem as they please (evergreen fund). Both funds have 10% of their assets in cash. The market is undergoing a severe correction and XYZ receives redemptions for 40% of its capital. XYZ will be able to satisfy 10% with cash, but will need to sell 30% of its portfolio at depressed market prices. On the other hand, ABC is not wasting time worrying about where they will find the capital to fund redemptions. They are analyzing the marketplace and using their 10% cash position to invest in companies at extremely advantageous prices. A year later, the stocks fully recover and investors in XYZ are in the red while those in ABC are taking their winnings to the bank.

It is therefore wise to understand the redemption terms of any fund you invest in. It is important to not only understand when you can get your own money out but also the degree of orderliness that would accompany a precipitous market decline.

5. Illiquidity

Illiquidity risk arises when investors are unable to convert their investments into cash at a fair price or at all. There are many factors that can cause an investment to become illiquid:

1. Lack of willing buyers
2. Lack of brokerage activity

3. Restrictive redemption terms

Much like volatility, which we discuss again later, illiquidity can be an investor's friend. **All other things being equal, assets that are illiquid generally provide a higher expected return than investments with more liquidity. If an investor has the flexibility to tolerate illiquidity, then he or she can earn compensation in the form of a higher return.**

One should not invest in illiquid assets if:

a) They require the money in the short term (i.e. buying a house in six months).

b) They are financing the purchase with debt that has a different maturity.

c) They are not fairly compensated for taking on the restriction of illiquidity.

If managers are leveraged or invested in illiquid assets, it is important for you to consider their cash position, and risk of illiquidity, as it relates to your own personal situation.

6. Business Risk

Whether you invest in stocks, bonds, real estate, or private equity, the underlying asset is some kind of business. Benjamin Graham, who we wrote about in Chapter Three, wrote how stock ownership represents a claim on the corporation's assets and earnings. If the business does well, so will you (assuming you don't pay too high a price – this is discussed next).

Business risk can arise in a wide variety of ways. Some examples include:

A. Company injects its capital structure with an unsustainable amount of debt, causing it to be sensitive to adverse conditions and go bankrupt.

B. Company sells a commodity product and they are undercut in price by a competitor.

C. Management makes poor strategic decisions that destroy shareholder value over time.

D. Company overpays for acquisitions.

When the price of one of your investments declines, it is important to make the distinction of whether it is a temporary decline, due to the normal fluctuations of the market, or a permanent decline, resulting from a change in the intrinsic value of the underlying asset.

7. Overpaying

The Nifty Fifty was a term that applied to fifty popular Blue Chip stocks during the 1960s and 1970s. These stocks were considered to be excellent buy and hold growth stocks. Many individual and institutional investors believed there was no risk in owning any of these companies and paid upwards of 60 and 70 times earnings to buy them. This valuation meant that, if all earnings went to shareholders, it would take 60 to 70 years for investors to recoup what they paid for the stock![1] As time showed in the 1970s, such valuations were unrealistic, as stock prices remained relatively flat or declined over the decade and many investors in the Nifty Fifty permanently lost what they had invested.

Recall the technology craze in the late 1990s. Technology, e-commerce, and the Internet had the potential to change how mankind existed. These companies were going to leave the world unrecognizable! Below are a couple of crazy and true stories from 1999:

- ❖ The average IPO after six months was selling for approximately 160% above its issue price on the very first day of trading!
- ❖ VA Linux, a company that distributed and serviced Linux operating systems, went public at $30 and saw its share price rise to a high of $320 before closing at $239.25 (697.5%) that day.
- ❖ Akamai had a market capitalization of $29 billion on $1.3 million of sales and negative $28 million of earnings.

There was no doubt that the world was changing, but, again, investors overpaid and permanently lost their capital. As Howard Marks put it, *"...it's one thing to innovate and change the world and another thing entirely to make money. Business will be different in the future, meaning that not all of the old rules will hold. On the other hand, profits come from taking in more in revenue than you payout in expense, and I don't think that's going to change."*[2]

During bubbles, investors do not worry about price because they are sure someone will pay a higher amount to buy from them later. Well, this works until it does not. You must never forget about the relationship between price and value. **The greatest capital destruction has occurred when investors bought companies that were considered perfect, or were expected to change the world, at prices that reflected that nothing could go wrong.**

8. Me, Myself, and I

Assume the following:

➤ You are an individual with a long investment horizon.

- You have no income requirement, the goal is steady capital appreciation.
- You have identified a company in a great business that has been able to grow earnings by 15% for the last 10 years.
- You have managed to buy the stock at a low price.

Guaranteed success, right? Not quite. Buying a great asset below its intrinsic value is half the battle. The other half is battling your own emotions. Let's say the shares of that company decline by 5%. Not a big deal, it is probably only market noise. Then it declines another 5%. You may be starting to get a little worried, but you still believe that the company is in good shape. And then two consecutive months of 10% declines. The company has lost 30% of its market capitalization and you are panicking. You can no longer convince yourself that the fundamentals of the business are strong. You are sure that your analysis was wrong and the market is right and you need to get out now before any further price declines!

Many people assume that investors act rationally, stock prices immediately incorporate all available information, and therefore assets are priced fairly. The truth is, more often than not, the market overreacts. Why? As we discuss in Chapter Nine, humans are only as logical as the biases that govern them. Research is increasingly revealing to us how physiological and psychological make-ups leave us susceptible to self-deceptions, biases, mental gaps, and a host of other human failings that distort our judgment.

9. Permanent Loss of Capital

The potential for a permanent loss of capital is the most important risk in investing. How could it not be? Surely that is scarier than seeing the volatility of your investment rise from 10% to 15%. A permanent loss of capital will occur when:

a) You take on excessive leverage and, one day, are forced to liquidate at distressed prices to meet a margin call.
b) You overpay for an asset.
c) The fundamentals of an asset deteriorate.
d) An investor lets emotions take over.

Consider the likelihood that you will see permanent loss in an investment and to what extent that may be. This is often difficult to do alone, and a trusted advisor can help.

It is clear that investment risk comes in many forms. Certain risks will matter to some investors but not to others. This leads us to the next question: Exactly how should one measure risk?

Part III: Measuring Risk

There are many investment professionals who believe risk can be computed and statistically manipulated. They depend solely on measures like the ones listed below to evaluate risk. Although these measures can be useful, using quantitative metrics devoid of thoughtful decision making is sure to yield disappointing results. Let us briefly examine these measurements and the rationale for using them:

- **Standard deviation (volatility):** Standard deviation is a measure of the dispersion of an asset's returns over time. A large (small) dispersion of returns tells us how much (little) the asset deviates. A larger standard deviation indicates that the returns will be more unreliable in the short term, and to some investors this unreliability poses risk.

- **Downside deviation:** One of the critiques of standard deviation is that it includes positive returns while investors are likely only worried about negative deviations. Downside deviation is the same as standard deviation except it only includes dispersion to the downside.

- **Value at risk (VaR):** VaR is a relatively new concept, being introduced to the investment world in the late 1980s. Now, the majority of institutional investors and hedge funds use VaR as part of their risk management system. VaR is a worst-case estimate of a portfolio's loss potential. One could calculate daily, monthly, or annual VaR numbers. For example, if a portfolio has a one-month 5% VaR of $25 million, this means that there is a 0.05 probability that the portfolio will decline more than $25 million in a month. Risk managers like VaR because it spits out a single statistical measure of the probability of loss, it is easy to interpret, can be quickly calculated, and can be used for all types of assets.

- **Beta:** In business school they teach you that to make more money you need to take bigger risks. And when you take on less risk, you get less return. The capital asset pricing model (CAPM) formula is used to depict this relationship (please excuse the odd symbols for a moment if you are not familiar with them):

$$r_a = r_f + \beta \, (r_m - r_f)$$

Where: r_a is the return on the asset; r_f is the return on a "risk-free" asset (i.e. 30-Year U.S. Treasuries); β is the beta of the asset; and $(r_m\text{-}r_f)$ is the market's return minus the return on the risk-free asset, also known as the "market premium."

This equation, which forms the basis of finance theory in universities and many large financial institutions, is read as *"the return on an asset is equal to the risk-free rate plus the <u>beta</u> of the asset multiplied by the market premium."*

In short, the CAPM formula asserts that an investor is compensated in two ways: (i) time value of money and (ii) risk. The risk free rate is the return an investor would earn for taking on no risk (i.e. investing in U.S. Treasuries), which is based on the time value of money. The next half of the equation measures the compensation required to take on additional risk. "Risk" is being defined as the asset's beta (a measure which denotes an asset's sensitivity to the broader market) multiplied by the market premium.

Because the risk-free rate and market premium are beyond the investor's control, CAPM implies that the only way to earn a higher return is to increase the beta, or risk. Moreover, this relationship is considered to be automatic: taking on more risk automatically leads to higher returns.

There are numerous shortcomings with the above-mentioned risk measures:

1. These measures typically assume returns follow predetermined distributions (patterns). However, history has shown that events which are prejudged to occur once in a thousand years can happen every decade. Predetermined patterns simply fail to predict the future. This simple idea is the subject of Nassim

Taleb's famous investing and epistemology book, *Fooled by Randomness*.

2. These measures typically do not take into account investment-specific attributes. For example: Company ABC makes computers and Company XYZ makes Barbie dolls. If ABC and XYZ have the same beta, then, according to CAPM, the one is as good (or bad) as the other. There is no analysis of the company's management, how the company makes money, whom their competitors are or if they have a sustainable competitive advantage, even though these factors play a major role in assessing risk.

3. Using beta as a measure of risk assumes that markets are efficient and prices always reflect the intrinsic values of companies. As we discussed in Chapter Three, this is not always the case. Assume on January 1st, Company ABC has a market capitalization of $100 million. Due to market fluctuations, on March 1st ABC's market capitalization decreases to $70M. Due to this sudden decrease, the beta of ABC increased and is now considered riskier than it was on January 1st. Think about it: you can now own ABC for $70 million instead of $100 million. Is paying less for a company riskier than paying more? Since prices can at times be "incorrect," a decline in price does not mean that the company has declined in value.

4. When it comes to mathematical models, the saying goes: "Garbage in, garbage out." VaR and other mathematically derived measures of risk are only as good as their inputs and assumptions. For example, if a mathematical model calculated value at risk as 10% but it assumed that asset prices would go on to double every year for the next decade, most of us would agree that the assumption is garbage and, as a result, the calculation of VaR as 10% is garbage. Although this is a stark

example, assumptions are always difficult to come up with and, more often than not, require estimation and judgment.

5. The risk measures listed above typically assume that historical relationships will hold. The most popular disclaimer that hedge fund managers use in their marketing material is "past performance is no indication of future performance." So why should past 'risk' be used as an indicator for future 'risk'?

The risks that really matter, such as a permanent deterioration in the fundamentals of an asset, paying too much for an asset, or mass redemptions during a chaotic market, to name a few, cannot be modeled. Models are only able to tell us what will happen under normal conditions; however, it is the extreme events that affect our portfolios the most

The Relationship Between Risk and Return

Recall that the Capital Asset Pricing Model (CAPM) assumes that return is directly and linearly dependent on how much risk (beta) we take. In order to achieve a higher return, you just need to take on more risk. The CAPM equation, when graphed, is represented by the straight line in the figure below:

$$r_a = r_f + \beta\,(r_m - r_f)$$

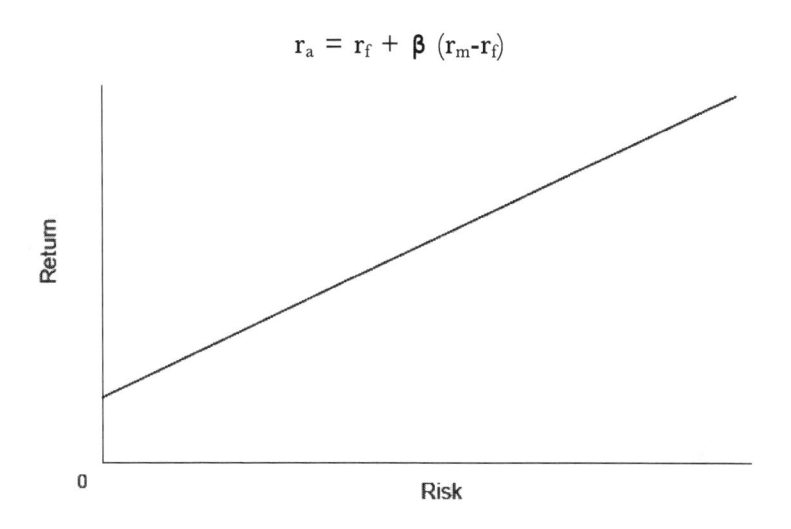

[Graph: Return (y-axis) vs Risk (x-axis), showing an upward-sloping line starting above 0.]

This popular graph is an overly simplistic representation of how investors should view risk. According to this equation and graph, all one needs to do is move rightward along the line above, increasing the risk (beta) and earning more in the process! Seems too good to be true, right?

Using CAPM as a point of reference, Oaktree Capital Chairman Howard Marks provides an excellent insight into the relationship between risk and return: *"In my opinion, especially in good times, far too many people can be overheard saying, 'Riskier investments provide higher returns. If you want to make more money, the answer is to take more risk.' But riskier investments absolutely cannot be counted on to deliver higher returns. Why not? It's simple: if riskier investments reliably produced higher returns, they wouldn't be riskier! The correct formulation is that in order to attract capital, riskier investments have to offer the prospect of higher returns."*[3]

Risk is not really about volatility and market sensitivity – it is about uncertainty. The traditional risk/return graph fails to incorporate the uncertainty associated with riskier investments. Riskier investments have higher expected returns and the potential for low returns/permanent losses. The graph on the next page, unlike the CAPM graph, shows a much more accurate representation of the relationship between risk and return.

At each point on the standard CAPM line (called the "security market line" or SML) the expected return cannot just be measured at a single point – since risk denotes uncertainty, there is a distribution of returns that are possible at each point. Naturally, the distribution is wider where uncertainty is greatest – and risk is highest – on the rightmost portion of the graph.

Given this understanding of risk, be careful if someone pitches you an idea based on the rationale that it's a good time to take risk because we're in a "risk-on" environment.

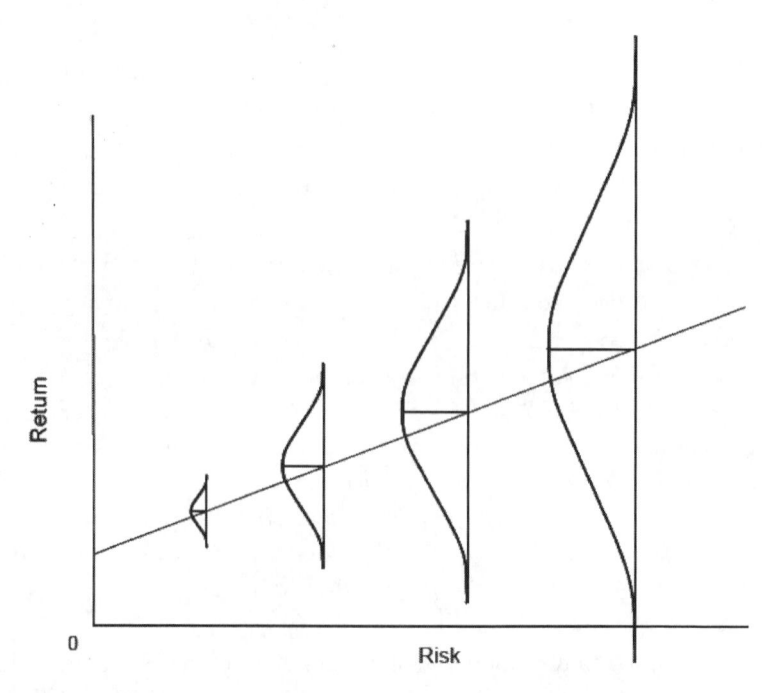

Marks, Howard. *The Most Important Thing: Uncommon Sense For The Thoughtful Investor.* New York: Columbia UP, 2011. p.34

Risk and Holding Periods

Another key aspect to risk is how long you intend to hold an investment. For example, if it is trading at a low price, the probability of permanently losing your capital in Coca Cola stock over a 15-year period is extremely low. On the other hand, day trading Coca Cola is very risky. Long-term trends need time to play out. This is something investors usually ignore. If you are investing in an asset that requires time to realize its full value, remember the six-foot-tall man who drowned crossing the stream that was five feet deep <u>on average</u>. He got about half way through, where it was twenty feet deep.

Understanding that risk is not the same as standard deviation, downside deviation, value at risk, or beta, eliminates the notion (deeply adored by academics) that risk is entirely quantifiable. A given investment may be risky for one investor but not another. Therefore, it is impossible for a single number to measure an investment's absolute riskiness. Will a pension fund fall short of its return objectives? Will a retiree have less than he needs to live his desired lifestyle? Will an investment fall in value and never recover? These are the real risks investors face. **As Leroy Dimson famously said, risk means more things can happen than will happen. Unfortunately, this is impossible to quantify or express through any one number.**

"Let the market be your servant, not your guide."

- Benjamin Graham

Part IV: Taking Advantage of Risk

As we discussed in Chapter Two, market sentiment, short time horizons and other factors cause investors to act irrationally and, in the process, create a volatile marketplace. Staying level-headed and diligent in such an environment can yield good investing opportunities.

Unable to stomach volatility, many investors decide to give up investing in public markets. These investors are choosing to sacrifice profit in exchange for lower volatility. At the time of this book's writing, interest rates are at historical lows. Investors buying Ten-Year U.S. Treasuries are accepting a yield of less than one-and-a-half percent. Rates are even lower in Germany, Japan and eight other countries. In the words of investor Whitney Tilson, "It is utter madness for long-term-oriented investors to accept such low interest rates... but institutional investors of the world are so scarred by stomach-churning volatility in the stock markets that they flee to islands of perceived safety."

If there is one takeaway from this chapter it is this: volatility is not your enemy. Under the right circumstances it is your best friend! Volatility creates opportunities to buy high quality assets at irrationally low prices. **Unlike in baseball where a batter has to swing at the pitches thrown, investors are free to ignore the price the market offers as many times as they please. The opportunity to buy mispriced assets, in our opinion, is a positive.**

At Berkshire Hathaway's 1997 shareholder meeting Warren Buffett spoke about volatility and Mr. Market: "...we'd probably make a lot more money if volatility was higher because it would create more mistakes in the market. Volatility is a huge plus to the real investor." Buffett then went on to explain Benjamin Graham's important concept of Mr. Market. Graham used the example of Mr. Market to view the stock market as a business partner who tends to oscillate between mania and depression and, depending on his mood, offers a price at which he will buy or sell. "The crazier he is, the more money you're going to make. So, as an investor, you love volatility."

Knowledge is Power

The more you know about what you invest in, the easier it is to stay calm when necessary and make informed and prudent decisions. It is important, therefore, to work hard to research and understand the value of the underlying assets you are buying. As Peter Lynch, one of Wall Street's most accomplished investors, once said, "Investing without research is like playing poker and never looking at the cards." This may seem rather obvious, but the truth is most investors do not understand what they are buying.

Imagine the founder of a small business. The founder knows the entire history of the company, exactly how the company makes money, how much cash is available for dividends or capital expenditures, who the main competitors are and where the opportunities exist. The founder has an excellent idea of what the company is worth. Say the founder would like to sell the business, but only at a fair price. Barring any unusual circumstances, the founder is not going to panic if he receives offers that are less than his estimate of what the company is worth. He will simply wait for an offer that he is pleased with. Investors should use the same mentality.

Investing more in an asset when its price has declined sharply is not difficult if you truly understand the asset's value. Ownership in a quality asset, purchased at a low price, will reduce the risk, or probability of permanently losing capital, of that investment. **Understanding the value of what you are buying is the most important thing in investing. Having a firm grasp of an investment's value allows you to stay the course when times get tough, take advantage of irrationally low prices, and do what so many investors fail to do – buy low and sell high.**

The Bottom Line

To recap, risk comes from:

- A. Not understanding the value of the asset you are buying.
- B. Overpaying for an asset, no matter how good you believe it is.
- C. Taking on excessive leverage.
- D. Investing in illiquid securities and having to liquidate immediately.
- E. Receiving notice of mass redemptions during a market collapse.
- F. Investing with a broker who is more worried about keeping his job than managing your portfolio.
- G. Emotions taking over and the irrational decisions that follow.
- H. Deterioration in the long-term fundamentals of an asset.
- I. The dynamic ever-changing world.

In the final analysis, risk is much more multi-faceted than many people give it credit for. It cannot be modeled or extrapolated with pinpoint accuracy. Certain risks matter to some investors but not others. Risk is simply an educated estimate of what the future holds. Riskier investments should offer the investor the potential for higher expected returns but also the possibility of lower returns and even losses. However, if you take the time to understand and analyze a given investment opportunity, and you trust the people you are partnering with, you will sleep well at night even as an irrational marketplace causes prices to wildly fluctuate.

"Once you become predictable, no one's interested anymore."

— *Chet Atkins*

Chapter Five
Spreading the Wealth
An Introduction to Asset Allocation

This chapter is the first of two that discuss asset allocation. You should be forewarned: This subject may be a bit dry. It is certainly not the sexiest side of investing. That being said, what it lacks in pizzazz, it compensates for in value. By going through this material (and staying awake while doing so), we believe the knowledge will be well worth your while. With that caveat, let us begin.

A person's "asset allocation" simply refers to the amount of different types of investments that he or she owns. For example, an investment portfolio with a traditional asset allocation might be 60% invested in public stocks and 40% invested in bonds. A broader asset allocation might include investments in real estate, commodities and private equity. In this sense, asset allocation is not something that is attained but rather something that is already present for all investors. Even an investor who has his or her entire net worth in cash has an asset allocation – their asset allocation is just 100% cash. Different types of investments (public stocks, bonds, cash, real estate) are referred to as "asset classes."

Not all asset allocations are created equal. Extensive effort should go into setting up the proper proportions of asset classes in order to meet the specific needs of the investor. Each asset class has specific characteristics. Some mainly produce income and others mainly provide long-term capital appreciation. Some react positively to inflation and others react negatively to inflation. The specific characteristics of each asset class are quite granular and are discussed in the next chapter.

In the meantime, this chapter provides an introduction to asset allocation. It discusses the role that asset allocation plays in the overall investment process and, just as importantly, what limitations it faces. Why do we put so much time into asset allocation? In what circumstances is it most important? These are the types of questions that are addressed in this chapter. They should be answered before delving into the often arduous and time-consuming asset allocation process. Ultimately, our hope is that, in reading the proceeding chapters, you will develop a working understanding of asset allocation and use that knowledge to make better investment decisions.

Part I: An Introduction to Asset Allocation

Asset allocation may best be described by giving it context. There are only three ways that an investor can make money – security selection, market timing and asset allocation. By understanding how asset allocation completes the trifecta of return-drivers, one can get a deeper understanding of what asset allocation really is. Security selection and market timing are, for better or worse, more familiar to most people than asset allocation.

Security Selection

Security selection refers to investing in specific securities[1] that one believes will go on to outperform other comparable securities. It involves the choice of specific assets within an asset class. Security selection is synonymous with "active" management because the manager actively picks out securities with the goal of beating the "passive" market index rate of return. For example, if someone is investing in large-cap U.S stocks, he or she can choose to invest in an index of the S&P 500 or certain companies that are contained in the S&P 500 (such as Proctor and Gamble, Walmart, and Coca-Cola). The latter choice involves security selection – picking certain stocks instead of the passive index. As we discuss in Chapter Seven, superior and sustained security selection is rare but can be an important source of investment returns.

Market Timing

Market timing involves investing (divesting) in anticipation of expected "booms" ("busts") in prices. It requires investing based on macroeconomic expectations.[2] For example, an investor might buy a stock or stock index based on his or her belief that over some time span, either minutes or years, the market will view it favourably and the price will increase. Day traders – investors who trade securities many times each day – derive all their investment returns from market timing.

Successful market timing is much rarer than successful security selection. There are literally thousands of macroeconomic variables that affect market prices and they all tend to act unpredictably. Isolating the variables that will dominate price changes, especially in the short-term, and then predicting their direction is a super-human feat. Taking transaction costs into consideration, pure market timing is almost always a losing strategy.

Asset Allocation

Asset allocation, the third driver of returns and the subject of the proceeding chapters, refers to selecting the proportions of asset classes that an investor holds in his or her portfolio. For the average investor, asset allocation is, by far, the most significant driver of returns. In one of the most famous studies about the role of asset allocation, Roger Ibbotson and Paul Kaplan found that, among mutual funds and pension funds, approximately 100% of returns were explained by differences in asset allocation policies.[3] As the authors point out, the result of their study is intuitive because, on average, security selection and market timing, which involve a transaction between two parties, result in a zero-sum game. When one side gains in a trade, the other side loses, so on average everyone breaks even.[4] Asset allocation, on the other hand, does not require someone else to be wrong in order for you to be right.

It is not only the average investor that is dependent on asset allocation policies for success. For 95% of mutual funds and pension funds, over 80% of returns are explained by differences in asset allocation policies.[5] The vast majority of investors depend on asset allocation policies to drive their returns and meet their needs.

The fact that asset allocation is the dominant source of returns for the vast majority of investors does not mean that all of one's investing effort should focus on asset allocation. As we mention many times throughout this book, focusing on investing with managers who can "beat the market" is an important source of value. However, the fact that asset allocation dominates returns certainly bodes well for investors who place it at the center of their investment process.

The Role of Diversification

An investor's asset allocation can range from being very narrow to very broad. An investor with a narrow asset allocation might have all their money invested in a single asset class or even a single asset. An investor with a broad asset allocation would invest across many different types of investments, covering several asset classes. At this point in our discussion the question remains: how broad should one's asset allocation be?

The word "diversification" describes the extent to which an asset allocation is broad or narrow. The broader a person's asset allocation is, the more diversified it is. The merits of diversification have become somewhat dogmatic in investment circles over the past 20 years. Modern Portfolio Theory, the theory that dominates academia and most professional finance circles, places diversification at the center of risk management. However, this train of thought is based on the idea that risk is the same thing as volatility. As we discuss in Chapter Four, however, risk and volatility are certainly not the same thing, so where does that leave diversification?

The Problem with Diversifying

There is a cost to diversifying across asset classes. Certain asset classes have better long-term prospects than others, and diversification requires diverting capital away from these options. In general, for example, equities tend to outperform bonds over very long time periods. Looking at the chart on the next page, it is clear that equities were a much better investment than fixed income over the 80-year period from 1925 to 2005. Whereas investors in Treasury bonds over this period multiplied their principal by 71 times, investors in large-cap stocks multiplied their principal by 2,658 times. The long-term returns of investors in small-cap stocks were even more favourable – much more.

This relationship makes sense, and will hold over long periods of time, because equity investors require greater compensation for the degree of risk they assume by being lower in the capital structure of companies compared to bondholders. Even the most recent decade, which has been one of the most difficult for equity investors in modern history, has done little to enervate this long-term relationship.[6] Any diversification away from equities and towards bonds leads to decreasing the returns one can expect over the very long term, so the reasons for diversification need to be compelling enough to offset that cost.

80-Year Wealth Multiples for U.S. Asset Classes and Inflation: *December 1925 – December 2005*

Asset Class	Multiple
T-Bills	18 times
Treasury Bonds	71 times
Corporate Bonds	100 times
Large-Cap Stocks	2,658 times
Small-Cap Stocks	13,706 times

Source: Swensen, David. Pioneering Portfolio Management. 2005.

There is also often a cost to diversify across assets, regardless of the different asset classes. Diversification requires investors to not only divert capital away from more favourable asset classes – it also requires investors to divert capital away from their highest conviction investment opportunities. Many of the most successful investors and businesspeople in history (some of whom are quoted in this book) abhorred diversification for this reason. From time to time, financial markets offer investors a fantastic opportunity – a "fat pitch" – and it can be costly and painful to abstain from putting all the eggs in that basket.

The Importance of Diversification

The merit of diversification is that it allows investors to retain access to investments that will behave differently as time goes on. When one asset class is doing poorly, other asset classes will not be affected and may, in fact, do very well. Different asset classes derive their value from unique sources, creating a situation in which there are few, if any, underlying commonalities among the different investments that one owns. As a result, diversification reduces an investor's dependency on the whims of any one asset class market. The result: Returns are less volatile and less uncertain over many years at a time.

Reducing volatility is important for two reasons, one emotional and the other practical. On the emotional side, reducing volatility has merit because, for the vast majority of people, watching their wealth decline by, say, 20% in a given year is traumatic, even if they know the decline is only temporary. Many of the people we speak to have spent decades building up their net worth, so watching a fifth of it disappear, albeit only the in short term, is something they very much want to avoid.[7] Different people have different preferences as far as their tolerance for volatility goes. There are significant advantages for embracing volatility but only if the person has the mindset to withstand it. In this light, diversification can help tailor one's investments to his or her personal preferences.

On the practical side, reducing volatility can increase long-term returns, even if it marginally reduces annual returns. This seemingly paradoxical relationship can be illustrated by a simple example: if an investment declines by, say, 20%, it must appreciate by 25% to get back to the value at which it started.[8]

Over time, this effect can have a meaningful impact, as illustrated in the following table. Even though the annual return for Investment A is higher by 1% on average, an investor in Investment B is better off after six years. A $1 million investment would turn into $1,601,613 in the former but $1,677,100 in the latter. Minimizing volatility for a marginal decline in annual returns is therefore incredibly useful for long-term investors, regardless of their personal tolerance for volatility.

Period	Investment A Return	Investment B Return
Year 1	30.0%	9.0%
Year 2	-10.0%	9.0%
Year 3	30.0%	9.0%
Year 4	-10.0%	9.0%
Year 5	30.0%	9.0%
Year 6	-10.0%	9.0%
Annualized Return	10.0%	9.0%
Cumulative Return	60.2%	67.7%

Decreasing the uncertainty of returns over many years is also very important for the vast majority of private investors. This is also achieved through diversification. In any given decade, any one asset class might be a bread-winner while the others lag behind. Looking at the chart on the next page, from January 1990 to January 2000, equities vastly outperformed bonds. An investment in the S&P would have nearly quintupled whereas an investment in the Lehman Aggregate Bond Index would have slightly more than doubled. However, from January 2000 to January 2010, bonds vastly outperformed equities. An investment in the S&P 500 would have declined slightly whereas an investment in the Lehman Aggregate Bond Index would have nearly doubled. The problem is, it is impossible to know which type of decade one is heading into at any point in time.

Spreading the Wealth

Decade	10-Year S&P 500 Return	10-Year Investment Grade Corporate Bond Return	Value of $1 Million After 10 Years of Equities	Value of $1 Million After 10 Years of Equities
Jan. 1990 - Jan. 2000	17.44%	8.11%	$ 4,990,688.00	$ 2,181,015.00
Jan. 2000 - Jan. 2010	-1.30%	6.69%	$ 877,347.00	$ 1,901,896.00

Most of us do not have the privilege of being able to lock away our money for decades at a time. Money is eventually called upon by most people to do one of many things, be it paying for a child's wedding, buying a summer residence, paying for health-care or providing income for standard month-to-month expenses. For these people, excessive uncertainty over a decade-long period about the degree to which their investments will provide a rate of return is not an option. For this reason, they must diversify.

Diversification among assets, and not just asset classes, is also important for protecting oneself against the randomness that pervades investing. Even if a fantastic opportunity – again, the "fat pitch" – comes along, most people need to hold back. The nature of randomness is such that it is possible to make "correct" decisions and be unsuccessful, just as it is possible to make "incorrect" decisions and be successful. Much like other things in life, the quality of the decision cannot be ascertained solely by the success of its outcome. To protect against this aspect of investing, it is prudent to diversify across various high-conviction opportunities rather than putting all of one's money in the highest-conviction opportunity.

In general, an investor should imagine what would happen to each investment under its worst-case scenario, and restrict the amount they invest in that opportunity based on that worst case being realized. For most people we speak to, this mental exercise results in having many modestly-sized[9] investment positions in high conviction opportunities. It takes a tremendous amount of work to put together such an investment portfolio, but the results are worth it.

Managing Diversification

Since diversification does come at a cost, it must be carefully managed in order to strike the appropriate balance. The goal of the diversifying investor is to maximize the benefits of diversification while minimizing its costs. Thankfully, by its nature, diversification allows for a disproportionately high decrease in volatility and uncertainty for a relatively small decrease in expected returns. This wonderful characteristic of diversification is often referred to as "the only free lunch" in finance.

The reason behind this effect is difficult to grasp without understanding the mathematics involved, so it is provided in Appendix A. In practice, however, research shows that investors have increased their returns for a given amount of volatility by diversifying across asset classes. The graph on the following page shows how an investor would have fared if he or she diversified across Treasury notes and the S&P 500 from 1950 to 2004. Intuitively, one might expect that a portfolio consisting of these two assets, in equal parts, would be as volatile as the average volatility of the two assets. This hypothetical performance is represented by Point B. In reality, however, the performance of this 50-50 portfolio is not at Point B – it is at Point A, where volatility is lower and the return is the same.

This relationship holds true when assets respond differently to the same market conditions, as is the case with stocks and Treasury notes. In times of crisis, when stock prices plummet, the prices of Treasury notes increase. For investors holding Treasury notes along with their stocks, the stock market declines are cushioned, reducing volatility in the process. This process occurs even though returns are not materially affected.

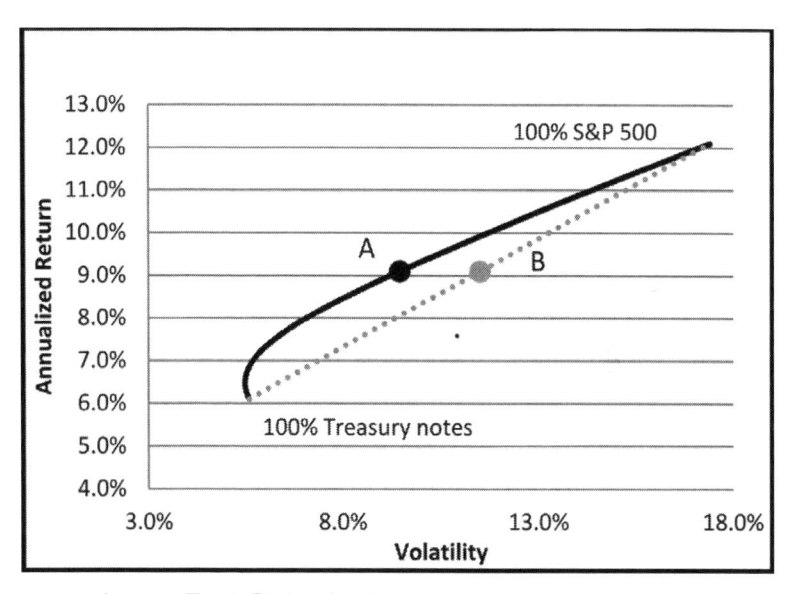

[Chart: Annualized Return vs. Volatility, showing curve from 100% Treasury notes to 100% S&P 500, with points A and B marked]

Source: Ferri, Richard. *All About Asset Allocation*, 2006.

For simplicity, our discussion has centered on stocks and bonds in the diversification process. In reality, there are many different types of investments: real assets, private equity, and "absolute return" assets, each of which is comprised of a nearly endless set of opportunities. Investors can also diversify across different types of countries, whether they are developed or emerging, Eastern or Western.

The question remains: what are the different asset classes and how do we define them? This question is answered in the next chapter. Although, frankly, cataloguing the different types of investments may not be the most riveting subject matter in and of itself, it is much more interesting than one might think. Defining the asset classes gets to the heart of the question of where each investment derives its value from. The key is that each asset class should derive its value from a unique source and should therefore behave differently from the others over time, thereby reducing volatility and uncertainty while maintaining strong investment returns.

The Bottom Line

Asset allocation is a very important part of the investment process. Among the three drivers of investment returns – security selection, market timing and asset allocation – the vast majority of investors' returns are determined by their asset allocation policies. Diversification, which is the extent to which a person's asset allocation is broad or narrow, is useful for reducing volatility and creating more certainty in expected returns over a given 10-year period.

The key to diversification is creating a portfolio in which different asset classes behave differently as time goes on, thereby protecting the investor from the whims of the market in any one particular asset class. Whereas under-diversification exposes investors to the risk that their returns are too volatile and uncertain, over-diversification exposes investors to the risk that their investment returns do not meet the required rate of return to meet their needs. Striking the ideal position between the two requires a delicate balancing act supported by the foundation of a thoughtful and disciplined investment process.

Asset allocation can and should extend beyond domestic stocks and bonds. There are thousands of different types of investment opportunities available for investors and these opportunities can be categorized into seven asset classes: (i) Domestic Equities, (ii) Foreign Equities, (iii) Government Guaranteed Fixed Income, (iv) Income-Driven Fixed Income, (v) Absolute Return, (vi) Real Assets and (vii) Private Equity. These asset class categories are the subject of the next chapter.

"Know what you own, and know why you own it."

- Peter Lynch

Chapter Six
Knowing What You've Got
Defining the Asset Classes

Now that we have outlined the need for proper asset class diversification, it's important to take a closer look at what actually defines and differentiates the asset classes.

This chapter, the second of two discussing asset allocation, delves deeper into the asset classes and answers the question: what exactly are these categories that we are dividing our investments into? Although this topic might seem impractical, or even pedantic, the way people define the asset classes can determine their degree of investment success. Definition occurs before the investment policy statement is created and, by that fact alone, determines the trajectory of the investment process. Like a person walking in a straight line for miles, taking a small turn one way or the other at the beginning leads to endpoints that are nowhere near each other. Poor definition causes a chain of events that ultimately results in poor execution and poor results.

The first part of this chapter outlines a paradigm for asset class definition. The main message is that asset class categorization should be based on the same goals that permeate the entire asset class diversification process. As we discussed in the last chapter, the whole point of diversification in the first place is to minimize volatility and 10-year uncertainty for as little of a decline in expected returns as possible. This intent should start at the first phase of the asset allocation process when we actually define each of the asset classes.

The second part of this chapter defines each of the asset classes according to the paradigm set out in the first part. Each of the asset classes, based on the definitions we outline, has a unique function and behaves differently from the others over time. This simple quality is the foundation upon which the entire asset allocation process is based. As different investments behave differently over time, investors are not subject to the whims of the market in any individual asset class. They can enjoy more consistent and predictable returns than they would otherwise have if they put all their money in just one asset class or one asset. The only way to know whether investments will behave differently over time, however, is to understand them at their deepest, most fundamental level: where they derive their value from (i.e. how they make money). Getting to the heart of the different types of investments is, therefore, a key part of defining the different asset classes.

The third part of this chapter links asset class definition to the actual allocation process. Proper asset class definition can help investors broaden their range of investment opportunities and, in the process, increase the benefits of diversification that we wrote about in the last chapter. Moreover, as we mentioned in the first chapter, broadening one's horizons in terms of what one is willing to invest in can help put a private investor in the same playing field as the most sophisticated and successful institutional investors. The third section also includes a visual of how such a portfolio might look and how different it is from the traditional private investor portfolio.

As we half-jokingly warned at the beginning of the previous chapter, this material is certainly not the sexiest side of investing. What it lacks in pizzazz, however, it abounds in usefulness. With that in mind, our hope is that this chapter will help you develop a deep understanding of the different types of investment opportunities out there and how they interact with each other. In the process, we hope that this knowledge will help you make better investment decisions.

A Paradigm for Asset Class Definition

The best asset class categorization is one that allows investors to reap the most benefit from asset class diversification. The same focus should permeate the whole investment process – from asset class definition to the actual implementation. Since the whole point of diversification is to minimize volatility and uncertainty while maintaining returns, asset classes should be defined in such a way as to reach that end-goal.

As we discussed in the last chapter, the only way to benefit from diversification is to have a cross section of different investments that will behave differently as time goes on. In this sense, one should not just arbitrarily separate each of the asset classes. Many investors divide asset classes according to the structure of the investment vehicle (i.e. ETF, mutual fund, hedge fund). These structural differences have little impact on the way that the investments will behave over time and, as far as asset allocation goes, are arbitrary. Instead, the function that each asset class plays in the portfolio context is the only basis of meaningful differentiation. If two investments will react in opposite ways to the same event, then they need to be placed in different asset classes. If they react similarly to the same event, then they need to be placed in the same asset class.

This process requires an understanding of the most fundamental elements of each investment. In order to get a good idea of how an investment will behave as time goes on, one must understand where it derives its value from. There are many different sources of value for different types of investments: cash flows from companies, prices of natural resources, borrowers paying their mortgages and the economic growth of emerging markets, to name a few. Whereas investments with the same source of value will behave similarly over time, investments with different sources of value will behave differently. As a result, different asset classes should have different sources of value.

Taken to the extreme, this framework would result in a nearly infinite number of asset classes. No two investments behave the same way all the time. The key is to balance pragmatism and accuracy in defining the asset classes. Whereas pragmatism favours a smaller, more manageable number of asset classes, accuracy favours having as many asset classes as possible. In the end, the optimal number is probably between six and nine asset classes, each one comprising no more than 35% and no less than 5% of the overall investment portfolio. Each asset class needs to be large enough to have an impact on overall returns but not too large as to dominate returns.

Putting this paradigm into action can help create an investment portfolio comprised of groups of assets that are differentiated at their most fundamental level. Putting all the parts together results in a portfolio with investments that will behave in different ways as time goes on, thereby reaping the benefits which diversification strives for in the first place.

Traditional vs. Alternative Assets

Asset classes can be divided into two broad groups: Traditional assets and Alternative assets. Traditional assets are characterized by what can be called "market exposure" — the returns that investors earn are primarily dependent on what happens in the broader market.[1] The Traditional asset classes are equities and fixed income. Dividing these categories a little finer, we get the four Traditional asset classes:

1. Domestic Equities
2. Foreign Equities
3. Government Guaranteed Fixed Income
4. Income-Driven Fixed Income

The Alternative asset classes are characterized by what is called "alpha," which is exposure to the expertise of the investment manager. The returns in the Alternative asset classes are primarily dependent on whether the investment manager uses his or her acumen to provide investors with profits. There is no "market" to outperform for Alternative assets. Any indexes that track market performance for Alternative assets tend to be uninvestable, unreliable or show very low long-term returns. Investors who profit by investing in Alternative assets over the long-term are those whose money is expertly managed.

Alpha is deeply related to market efficiency, which is the subject of Chapter Three. In short, Alternative assets operate in markets where intelligent, informed, diligent and objective investors have a particularly large edge over the competition and, in the process, provide returns that are not dependent on what happens in the overall financial market. The Alternative assets are divided into the following asset classes:

5. Absolute Return
6. Real Assets
7. Private Equity

Alternative assets provide meaningful diversification benefits because they can provide investors with returns that, by definition, behave differently from the overall market. Alternative assets have the propensity to go up regardless of whether the broader financial markets are going up or down. Even though these assets sound perfect, they may be subject to their own market fluctuations and, during times of booming stock markets, tend to underperform equities.

Despite the differences between Traditional and Alternative assets, the fundamental analysis remains the same: The goal of the investor is to buy assets below their intrinsic value.[2] The main difference is that Alternative assets derive their value primarily from the person managing the assets whereas Traditional assets derive their value primarily from the power of the market.

Taken together, the seven asset classes cover the gamut of investment opportunities in the world. As the rest of this chapter makes clear, each one derives its value from a unique source and therefore behaves differently as time goes on. Depending on the investor's wants and needs, different proportions of each type of investment should make up the overall portfolio.

The Asset Classes

Asset class definition is as much of an art as it is a science. As you will see when reading through this section, there is some heterogeneity within each asset class. Taken as a whole, however, this categorization balances the accuracy and pragmatism issue that we mentioned earlier.

The descriptions of each asset class here are narrow in scope – entire books have been written about each one. In the process, a degree of detail is not included. That being said, the descriptions can provide the reader with an understanding of how defining the asset classes in this way creates groups of investments that derive their value from different sources and behave differently over time, thereby allowing investors to reap the benefits of diversification.

Domestic Equities

Domestic equities include publically-traded securities that provide investors with ownership over pieces of corporate North America. Relative to other asset classes, domestic equities are very liquid and heavily researched. The North American equity market is one of the largest financial markets in the world. The NYSE, NASDAQ and TSE combined have a market capitalization of over US$20 trillion. As we discussed in the last chapter, domestic equities have historically, over the long-term, provided investors with higher capital appreciation than any of the other asset classes. Moreover, stock returns tend to increase during periods of inflation. As a result, domestic equities provide protection against eroding purchasing power over time.

Despite the overall market being relatively efficient compared to others, it is possible to outperform with expert active management. Focusing on the least efficient segments of the market – small-capitalization stocks – augurs well for investors using active management for their domestic equity exposure. With fundamental research by investment managers, the domestic equity allocation may bear little resemblance to the broader market and there will be short-term deviations from market returns. Focusing solely on the long term, especially when other market participants are short-term focused, can be of tremendous value to equity investors.

Foreign Equities

Foreign equities include publically-traded securities that provide investors with ownership of pieces of corporations outside of

North America. There are two types of foreign equity investments: those in developed countries and those in emerging countries. Although there are differences between these two sub-categories, they are combined within the same asset class because their function within an investment portfolio is the same. Investments in the foreign equities asset class provide investors with long-term capital appreciation in markets that will behave differently over time from the domestic equity market. Different economies around the world not only specialize in different industries but also operate under different regulatory environments. Heavily regulated economies may restrict international companies' access to their local consumers, creating a unique source of returns for their companies.

Equities in emerging economies usually trade in less efficient markets than equities in developed economies. There may be uncertainty regarding financial statements, local infrastructure and business culture. Almost all emerging markets have, at some point or other, experienced a hiatus in trading activity due to financial crises.[3] As a result of these additional risks, investors should demand a higher rate of return for investing in such markets. As the global economy progresses, however, emerging markets are becoming less subject to uncertainty as countries such as India, China, Russia, South Korea, Brazil, and Mexico are developing at an unprecedented pace.

Government Guaranteed Fixed Income

Government Guaranteed Fixed Income includes a narrow range of fixed income securities that are guaranteed by the largest, highest credit-quality bodies in the world. Securities included in this asset class are U.S. Treasuries and bonds backed by AAA credit rated governments. Also included in this category are "Agencies" – bonds issued by government agencies such as the Government National Mortgage Association (Ginnie Mae) – as well as bonds issued by Government Sponsored Entities (GSEs) such as The Federal National Mortgage Association (Fannie Mae) and the Federal Home Loan Mortgage Corporation (Freddie Mac). Agencies and bonds issued by GSEs are, either implicitly or explicitly, backed in full-faith by the credit of the United States Government. Taken as a whole, Government Guaranteed Fixed Income includes assets that are commonly referred to as "Risk-Free Assets." [4]

Of course, after reading Chapter 3 of this book, you know that these assets are not "risk-free" in the sense that investors have nothing to worry about if they invest in them. Rather, these assets provide two things: reliable income and protection against catastrophe in financial markets. Government Guaranteed Fixed Income provides investors with comparatively low interest payments but an unparalleled degree of certainty that payments will be made. Of equal importance, these securities are treated as a safe-haven for the vast majority of investors when markets take a turn for the worse. Investing in this asset class can therefore cushion any draw-downs that may occur in the rest of an investor's portfolio when a financial catastrophe hits. Moreover, as a result of the reliable interest income and unparalleled liquidity of Government Guaranteed Fixed Income securities, this asset class can provide cash for portfolio operations or income for the investor's month-to-month expenses. The downside of this asset class is that, historically, over very long periods of time, it provides investors with the lowest rate of return. In this light, Government Guaranteed Fixed Income should comprise only the minimum amount necessary in order to provide liquidity for portfolio operations and protection against financial catastrophe/malaise.

Income-Driven Fixed Income

Income-Driven Fixed Income is the last of the four Traditional asset classes. This asset class includes securities that provide investors with regular income, although without the hedging quality or reliability of Government Guaranteed Fixed Income. Investments included in this asset class are corporate bonds, mortgages, structured credit and other income-producing securities. Both "investment grade" and "high yield" securities can fall into this asset class.

These securities offer a higher rate of return than Government Guaranteed Fixed Income as a result of the risks that (i) the borrower may default, (ii) the investor may not be able to trade the securities whenever they want to and/or (iii) some option embedded in the security may result in it being taken away from the investor at an inopportune time.[5] For investors that require a provision of income in their portfolio, Income-Driven Fixed Income may be a core position. Since bondholders have priority over equity holders when it comes to payments coming out of a company, securities in this asset class are subject to less uncertainty than securities in the equity asset classes.

Absolute Return

The Absolute Return asset class is the first and quite possibly the quintessential Alternative asset class. As its name denotes, this asset class includes investments for which returns are derived completely independently of the ups and downs of any financial market. Generally, this asset class contains investments that are less familiar to most people and require strategies dependent on the expertise of the investment manager. The four categories of Absolute Return strategies are: Event Driven, Value Driven, Quantitative Trend-Following and Global Macro. For the curious reader who is interested in knowing more about these strategies, detailed descriptions are provided in Appendix B. The unifying characteristic of these investments is that financial markets play little to no role in determining returns.

The Absolute Return asset class has received increased attention over the past 20 years. In the process, the hedge fund industry has emerged from obscurity as virtually all major institutional investors have increased allocations to its strategies.[6] For many investors, returns that are uncorrelated to the general market seem idyllic, especially in light of the lackluster returns earned by most investors in the equity market during the first decade of the 21st Century. Although Absolute Return investments are an extremely important source of diversification, investors must remember that its strategies are still subject to the uncertainty that is present in all investing. The advantage of the asset class is that its behaviour is unique from that of other asset classes. Since the investments derive their fundamental value from a unique source – specifically, whoever the investment manager is – they will behave differently than the other asset classes over time and, in the process, provide the benefits of asset allocation that we have spoken about throughout the past two chapters.

Real Assets

Real assets include investments in physical properties such as real estate, infrastructure and natural resources. One of the most important qualities of real assets is that they provide income streams that tend to track inflation. Since real assets provide important goods and services to people, their income streams tend to increase as the prices of goods and services in the general economy increase. From an investor's standpoint, real assets provide protection against the purchasing power erosion that occurs during inflationary periods.

Another equally important quality of investments in this asset class is that there are particularly significant opportunities for investors to exploit market inefficiencies and, in the process, earn returns that are dependent on manager expertise rather than market momentum. It surprises many people to learn that the long-term capital appreciation of real estate, even in central urban locations, for example, is no greater than the historical rate of inflation.[7] The degree to which investors are able to profit from investing in real estate is dependent on when they buy and how well they develop or operate the property. A similar situation exists for infrastructure and natural resources. Whereas long-term market-driven capital appreciation proves elusive, outsized investment returns are available for investment managers who have particular expertise in the area.

Private Equity

Private Equity is the last of the seven asset classes and rounds out our descriptions of the different types of investment opportunities. Private Equity includes ownership over pieces of companies that do not trade on public exchanges such as the NYSE or TSE. The asset class can be subdivided into two categories: buyouts and venture capital. Buyouts are private equity transactions in which the investors purchase ownership in a company that is already mature. Venture capital refers to private equity transactions involving young, newly created companies. Similar to the other Alternative asset classes, the key source of value-creation is manager expertise rather than market momentum. In the case of venture capital, the investor's returns depend on management's ability to develop operations effectively. In the case of buyouts, the investor's returns depend on management's ability to adjust operations effectively. Whereas many private equity transactions predominantly focus on financial engineering and leverage rather than operational change, such strategies are speculative and generally inadvisable.

Private Equity is characterized by low liquidity and high expected returns. In many cases, returns are particularly uncertain because operational changes can cause states of flux within a company. Even in the simplest buyout transactions in which few operational changes need to be made, the mere act of changing ownership over a company can derail a company if it is not handled carefully. The upside to assuming this risk is that private equity can be a strong driver of returns for the overall investment portfolio. Moreover, these returns behave differently over time than the rest of the market because they have a unique source of value and, as a result, behave independently, allowing investors to benefit from diversification.

Broadening Your Investment Horizons

In the first chapter of this book, we wrote about the benefits of investing across a broader range of investment opportunities, which is a notion integrally linked to the asset class definitions in this chapter. Listing the different types of investments available to investors can help people to realize where they need exposure and where they may be over-exposed. It can help with idea generation as well as risk management. Rather than just thinking about asset classes as "equity" and "fixed income" as most private investors do, these definitions help people evaluate the full breadth of investment opportunities.

It is important not only to invest across a broad range of asset classes but also to invest across the plethora of strategies within each asset class. This also increases the benefits of asset class diversification because it incorporates investments that behave differently from one another over time.

Using words alone, it is difficult to picture how dramatically different such a portfolio might be from your traditional asset allocation. With that in mind, the pie charts on the next pages provide a vision for high-net-worth private investors of what their investment portfolio could be if they were willing to broaden their horizons and insist on having access to a wider range of opportunities. Charts A and B provide an overview of the asset class diversification and Charts C and D provide a deeper analysis of the same asset allocations divided by strategy.[8] Using the ideas discussed in this chapter, an investor interested in reaping the benefits of diversification would clearly prefer the Opportunity-Rich Private Portfolio to the Traditional Private Portfolio. The former is comprised of a much wider range of investments with unique sources of value that will behave in different ways as time goes on. In the process, an investor with such a portfolio has lower volatility and 10-year uncertainty with equal or greater expected returns.

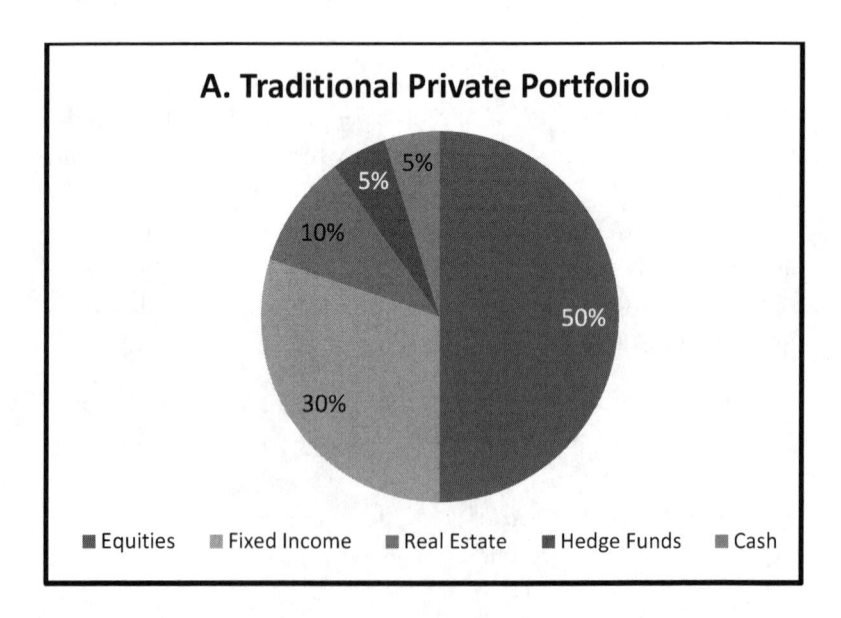

A. Traditional Private Portfolio

- Equities: 50%
- Fixed Income: 30%
- Real Estate: 10%
- Hedge Funds: 5%
- Cash: 5%

B. Opportunity-Rich Private Portfolio

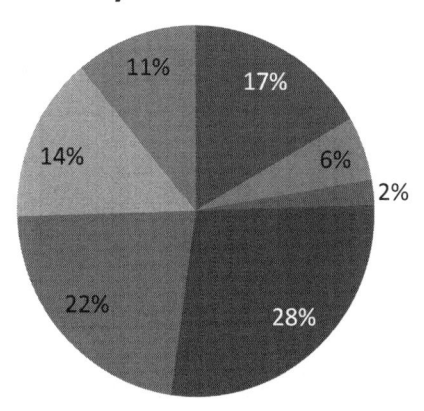

- 17%
- 6%
- 2%
- 28%
- 22%
- 14%
- 11%

- Domestic Equities
- Foreign Equities
- Government Guaranteed Fixed Income
- Income-Driven Fixed Income
- Absolute Return
- Real Assets
- Private Equity

C. Traditional Private Portfolio

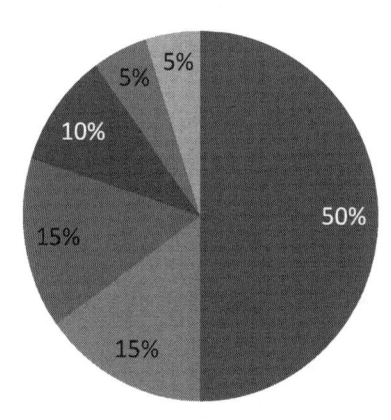

- 50%
- 15%
- 15%
- 10%
- 5%
- 5%

- Large-cap Equities
- Government Guaranteed Fixed Income
- Investment Grade Fixed Income
- Domestic REITS
- Long-short Equity
- Cash

D. Opportunity-Rich Private Portfolio

- Mid-cap Domestic Equties (3%)
- Small-cap Domestic Equities (8%)
- Foreign Equities (5%)
- Government Guaranteed Fixed Income (2%)
- Investment Grade Bonds (5%)
- High Yield Bonds (8%)
- Structured Credit (5%)
- Private Debt and Mortgages (8%)
- Long-short Equity (6%)
- Arbitrage Strategies (3%)
- Quantitative Trend Following (3%)
- Global Macro (3%)
- Distressed Debt (3%)
- Distressed Equity (5%)
- Domestic Real Estate (3%)
- Foreign Real Estate (3%)
- Infrastructure (3%)
- Natural Resources/Commodities (3%)
- Private Equity Investment #1 (3%)
- Private Equity Investment #2 (3%)
- Private Equity Investment #3 (10%)
- Cash (3%)

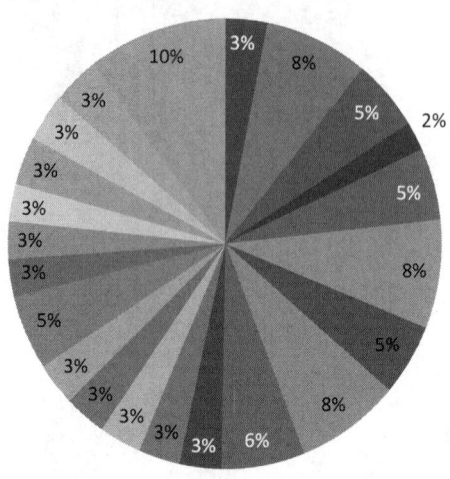

The Bottom Line

Using the information contained in this chapter, you can develop a deeper understanding of each of the asset classes and how they work together to form an investment portfolio with less volatility and uncertainty of returns. Unfortunately, this subject is relatively dry (at least for most people), but the contents herein address many important practical concerns for people using asset class diversification in their investment process.

One thing we did not write about in this chapter is the amount that one should allocate to each of the asset classes. Although many authors and professionals have expressed their notions of the "perfect" asset allocation, we believe that such thinking is not just a waste of time but potentially damaging. The proportion of money placed in each asset class must be specific to the needs and wants of the investor. Each asset class carries with it unique attributes – both in terms of risk and return – and these attributes must align with the people putting their money on the line. As a result, deciding on the appropriate asset allocation requires time and effort, culminating, for most people, in an Investment Policy Statement (IPS). As we discussed in Chapter 2, such soul searching cannot be delivered or mass produced but is rather part of an ongoing process in which the investor must be an active participant.

"Success is found where opportunity meets preparation."

- Henry Hartman

Chapter Seven

The Art and Science of Manager Selection

Since the day Prime Quadrant was created, we have selected outside investment managers to manage our clients' money rather than providing such services "in-house" (i.e. owning proprietary investment products). Manager selection is one of our most important roles. Since the different types of investment managers are virtually endless in number, we put considerable time, thought and effort into investment manager selection. In that light, we want to take the opportunity to share our thoughts with you on how high-net-worth individuals and families can go about fulfilling this important step in the investment process.

It is first important to explain what we mean by "investment managers." Investment managers, as we define them, are companies or individuals that (i) aggregate money belonging to many investors *and* (ii) invest the money within a specific asset class that the manager specializes in. For example, one investment manager might be a hedge fund that invests in North American mid-sized companies. Another might be a real estate fund that buys commercial properties in large Asian cities. There are different funds for virtually every investment strategy imaginable. Our job is to sift through the different categories of investment managers as well as different investment managers within each category. In the process, the goal is to determine which managers best serve each individual's (or, in our case, each client's) specific situation.

This chapter is separated into two parts. The first part provides some background on the importance of selecting not just any investment managers but the <u>right</u> investment managers. As this chapter will discuss, selecting anyone but the top performing investment managers leads to results that are (in best cases) a waste of time or (in most cases) a waste of time and money. Unfortunately, it is impossible to know which investment manager will go on to outperform all of their competitors. However, there are certain guidelines that one can follow to select managers that are likely to perform within the top quartile (or, better yet, the top decile!) of their peers and compensate investors for the time, effort and fees required to invest with them.

The second part of this chapter outlines our investment manager selection process from the beginning stages – when we first learn about a manager – to the final stages – when we monitor performance and decide, on a continuous basis, whether to stay invested.

As with most things in investing, there is a combination of quantitative and qualitative factors that go into the decision-making process. Software programs allow investment professionals to evaluate portfolios under various assumptions and scenarios. Lacking the almighty crystal ball as we do, such analysis is important but limited. The use of quantitative methods devoid of thoughtful decision-making leads to portfolios that are sure to yield undesired results. Since the quantitative side of investment manager selection is generally too technical for this book, we will mostly stick to the qualitative side of things. (You're welcome!) The qualitative side, however, is no walk in the park. With some time and energy, we hope that at least a few of the ideas in this chapter will ring true to you and, ultimately, help you make better investment decisions.

1. The Importance of Selecting the Right Investment Managers:

A Little Difference Goes a Long Way

Throughout this section we make reference to managers who over- or under-perform their benchmark indexes by as little as 1% to 2% per year. This seemingly minute amount begs the question: how big of a difference does 1% to 2% per year actually make?

Although small percentage differences in the short-term may seem relatively insignificant, the long-term effect of even marginal over- or under-performance is staggering. The reason for the large effect of small differences in investing is due to what Albert Einstein allegedly described as the most powerful force in the universe: compound interest. The following chart shows the impact of seemingly insignificant differences in annual returns over 15 years.

Annual Return	Investment	Year 5	Year 10	Year 15	Additional Wealth
Base Case: 4%	$10,000,000.00	$12,166,529.00	$14,802,443.00	$18,009,435.00	N/A
5%	$10,000,000.00	$12,762,816.00	$16,288,946.00	$20,789,282.00	*$2,779,847.00*
6%	$10,000,000.00	$13,382,255.00	$17,908,477.00	$23,965,581.00	*$5,956,146.00*

After 15 years, an investment of $10 million earning 4% a year compounded is worth just over $18 million. This type of return would in all likelihood outpace inflation and protect a person's purchasing power (which is by no means something to scoff at, especially in light of our most recent decade's market returns). A 1% and 2% outperformance over this base case, however, yields an additional $2.78 million and $5.96 million, respectively, by year 15. In other words, over a 15-year period, a 2% annualized outperformance translates into a 60% cumulative outperformance!

The effects of compound interest go both ways. A 2% under-performance is detrimental to the same extent that a 2% out-performance is beneficial. If an investor allocates to a manager who goes on to be out-performed by the passive index (like the S&P 500) by 2% a year, then, using the example above, that investor effectively losses almost $6 million of his or her money.

When it comes to investment returns, the margins are small but the stakes are high. As a result of the "miracle" of compounding, little differences go a long way. So how good are managers at providing the little differences to their investors? As the next section discusses, investment manager out-performance is more elusive than most believe.

The Bad News: Even Little Differences are Hard to Come By

Selecting investment managers is not for the casual consumer or the faint of heart. The main issue for investors looking to get their money's worth investing in active funds is that, over the long-term, the average investment manager underperforms the no-fee benchmark index[1]. As a result, investors in the average fund are consistently better off forgoing the whole investment manager selection process and just putting their money in an index.

Investment Manager Performance: 1995-2005

	Benchmark Index Return	First Quartile Manager[2]	Median Manager	Third Quartile Manager	Estimated Fees	Median Relative Return
U.S. Fixed Income	6.9%	7.2%	6.9%	6.7%	0.4%	-0.4%
U.S. Equity	9.9%	10.4%	9.5%	8.5%	0.8%	-1.2%

Source: Swensen, David. *Pioneering Portfolio Management*. 2005.

The data paint a bleak picture for investors allocating to their run-of-the-mill investment manager. The median (middle) performing investment manager in the two largest asset classes – U.S. fixed income and U.S. equities – did not perform well enough over the 1995-2005 period to warrant the fees they charged. Investors underperformed by investing with them. Taking a deeper look, in fixed income, even the top quartile investment manager provided clients with a losing strategy over the 10-year period. The time span from 1995 to 2005 is not unique. The average investment managers in the largest asset classes simply fail to earn their keep over time. Only the top performing investment managers provide a worthwhile service.

Investors can earn superior returns if they are able to discern which managers will go on to significantly outperform their peers, but these managers are surprisingly scarce. This insight brings us to **Investing Rule #1: when investing in the Traditional asset classes, only allocate to an investment manager if you are convinced the manager will go on to beat its peers by a wide margin.**

There is an intuitive explanation for these data explaining investment manager performance in Traditional equities and fixed income. The most popular asset classes are the ones in which managers have the biggest headwind in trying to "beat the market." Take the international fixed income market for sovereign bonds, for example. In this market, investors try to decide which country's sovereign debt is the cheapest or most expensive and weigh their portfolios accordingly. The problem for investment managers in this market is that the phenomena that determine the bond prices are among the most monitored phenomena in the world. Getting an edge over the competition under such circumstances is exceptionally difficult.

The source of disparity in top quartile performance among asset classes is the relative "efficiency" of each market. Market "efficiency" has to do with the number of independent investors who buy and sell from each other and how easily information flows among them. The more efficient a market is, the harder it is for managers to beat the competition because there is a more equal playing field. The opposite is true for less efficient markets.[2]

As the next section clarifies, not all asset classes are created equal. Investment manager performance in alternative asset classes paints a different picture for active managers.

Outside the Mainstream Markets (but Maybe Less than You Think):

Investment managers are not restricted to markets that are closely monitored by legions of institutional investors. There are other asset classes that attract significantly less attention than do Traditional fixed-income and equities. Investment managers operating in less efficient markets have the opportunity to make outsized gains (or losses) relative to other investors. The following table depicts this reality:

Investment Manager Performance: 1995-2005

	First Quartile Manager[4]	Median Manager	Third Quartile Manager	Range
U.S. Fixed Income	7.4%	7.1%	6.9%	0.5%
U.S. Large-Cap Equity	12.1%	11.2%	10.2%	1.9%
International Equity	10.5%	9.0%	6.5%	4.0%
U.S. Small-Cap Equity	16.1%	14.0%	11.3%	4.8%
Absolute Return	15.6%	12.5%	8.5%	7.1%
Real Estate	17.6%	12.0%	8.4%	9.2%
Leveraged Buyouts	13.3%	8.0%	-0.4%	13.7%
Venture Capital	28.7%	-1.4%	-14.5%	43.2%

Source: Swensen, David. *Pioneering Portfolio Management.* 2005.

This table shows just how different an environment investment managers operate in when they focus on different asset classes. Looking at the rightmost column, you can see that the range between the first-quartile managers and the third-quartile managers increases dramatically as we move from more popular asset classes to less popular asset classes. In the more popular asset classes, getting a significant edge over the competition is rare. At the same time, falling behind the competition is rare as well. The difference between the first- and third-quartile managers is therefore small. As investors get into the less mainstream asset classes such as small-cap equity, real estate and private equity (comprised of leveraged buyout and venture capital), the difference between the high-performing managers and the low-performing managers increases. This insight brings us to **Investing Rule #2: if one believes in his or her ability to select top-quartile managers in a given asset class, then that person is better off looking at managers in less traditional asset classes.**

The Importance of Selecting the Right Managers

Putting the two investing rules together, we can develop a comprehensive prescription for investors interested in allocating to investment managers. On the one hand, investors should abhor needlessly paying fees and allocating to average or sub-average investment managers. On the other hand, since small differences in annualized performance lead to big differences in cumulative performance, there is tremendous value in selecting investment managers that go on to outperform the rest. Due to the different degrees of market "efficiency" in the different asset classes, the benefits (costs) of selecting out-performing (under-performing) investment managers in less traditional asset classes is even greater. The only way to balance all these issues is to adopt a thoughtful and tested investment manager selection process that isolates the bread-winners and weans out the laggards. This process is the focus of the rest of this chapter.

The Good News: There is a Process to Help Select Managers

The rest of this chapter goes on to discuss how investors can go about selecting investment managers who will look over their assets in such a way as to serve their best interests. As Warren Buffett has often said, and we have often repeated, investing is simple but it is not easy. Many of the ideas in the rest of this chapter are incredibly intuitive and straightforward – they are merely challenging to implement because of the discipline required to adhere to them. Like fine wine, a good investment portfolio takes time and patience, and in the sometimes volatile landscape of investing, such traits can be in short order. As the saying goes, casual commitments invite casual reversals. Seriously committing to a trusted process, such as the one outlined in the rest of this chapter, can help one stick to his or her guns amidst the public melee that, from time to time, engulfs financial markets and causes people to divert from their best interests.

2. The Investment Manager Selection Process

In Atul Gawande's now famous book, *The Checklist Manifesto*, the author discusses how the sheer volume of information that faces decision-makers necessitates a form of simplification that can break complex problems down into manageable components. What could possibly be simpler than a checklist? (Ask any grocery shopper). Investments are no exception to the information-overload problem that faces many buyers. In fact, investing can often epitomize the information-overload problem.

As Bruce Greenwald, well-known investing expert and professor at Columbia Business School has said, "When you mix bad information with good information, you get bad information!" Forming and following a checklist is an excellent way to sift out bad information and focus on only those facts which are relevant to the end decision.

With this understanding in mind, the structure of this section follows a checklist format. Each item on the checklist is a question and, in totality, the questions culminate in the ultimate question at hand: to invest or not to invest? Answering each question takes time and effort but does not, by any means, require the highest IQ in the room. So without further ado, checklist item number one...

Does the investment strategy make sense?

With the proliferation of the hedge fund industry over the past 20 years, a plethora of new investment options have become available to the public. Today, investment strategies range from the traditional (i.e. buying public stocks) to the exotic (i.e. various arbitrage strategies) and encompass innumerable different ways that people are trying to make a buck or two. The downside of all this is that many of the more exotic investment options are too difficult (or non-sensible) to understand. People should never partake in investments they do not understand, no matter how enticing they may seem and how much money investors have made in the recent past. The reason? All too often, when things seem too good to be true, they are. **The only way to protect against getting caught up in a poorly conceived – or worse, fraudulent – investment scheme is to understand exactly how the investment managers make money and avoid losing money.**

Before 2009, Stanford International Bank operated out of the small Caribbean island of Antigua. The bank's founder and CEO, Allen Stanford, promised investors guaranteed returns in excess of 10% per year through the bank's certificates of deposit. How was it possible to provide such high "risk-free" returns? The underlying economics were suspiciously vague and unspecified. Still, Stanford was able to amass over $8 billion of assets from clients all over the world, including some of the most highly regarded investment professionals in their respective markets. The more "smart money" that went into the bank over time, the more money came flowing in behind it. By the end of February 2009, the company was charged with fraud and the SEC had filed official charges against the bank. Three years later, Allen Stanford was sentenced to 110 years in prison for orchestrating one of the largest Ponzi schemes in history. If people had asked the simple question, "How do you make money and not lose money?" and then made their investment decision conditional on receiving a good answer, then the scheme could have been avoided.

Warren Buffett is often quoted as saying that he has only two rules for his managers, "Rule No.1: Never lose money. Rule

No.2: Never forget rule No.1." Similarly, we often say that we are in the "stay rich business" rather than the "get rich business." **In the stay rich business, avoiding the permanent loss of capital is paramount to everything else. The goal is to hit singles and doubles, interspersed with the occasional home run.** Given this goal, it is necessary to ensure that the investment strategies are crystal clear. One should never over-reach into strategies outside one's circle of competence, even if this requires forgoing the prospect of making money.

Whereas permanently losing capital is completely unacceptable, losing out on opportunities beyond the scope of understanding is just an unfortunate but necessary part of the job description. Thankfully, there are many ways to make money (and not lose money) that make perfect sense to reasonably smart people willing to put in the effort.

Does the investment address a need for me?

Even the most compelling investment in the world should be foregone if it is not appropriate for the person investing. In a proper asset allocation process, investors should have a certain quota ("bucket") for each type of investment, each one sized according to the proportion that it should take up in the portfolio.[3] If the "bucket" is full, then there is no need for the investment and choosing to invest would just lead to a skewing of the portfolio away from its stated objectives. If, however, a person needs additional exposure to a particular asset class, then finding a worthwhile investment manager whose strategy addresses that need is incredibly valuable.

Every person has different needs – whether they relate to their tolerance to certain types of risk, their level of understanding, their need for short-term cash or any number of variables that should be brought into the investment process. Deciding whether a given investment fits any number of these needs requires attention. The result is a portfolio filled with investments, each of which has a specific function.

Does the portfolio manager exhibit the necessary characteristics for success?

Character is the most important (and yet the most overlooked) variable to consider when deciding whether to invest with a particular investment manager. Who are these people that you are placing your money with? Are they honest, thoughtful, independent-minded? Investors often forget that there are human beings behind the scenes, and that these people invariably determine the degree of investment success. In the words of David Swensen, Chief Investment Officer at the Yale University Endowment and the most successful institutional investor of the past two decades, "Nothing matters more than working with high-quality partners. Integrity tops the list of qualifications."

No matter how iron-clad or sophisticated investment terms may be, there is always the possibility, indeed a likelihood, that the interests of the investor and the interests of the investment manager will diverge at some point in time. An investment manager has to have character such that he or she is driven not only by money. Many great managers, for example, have an innate drive to put capital to work. They may be eccentric and have an independent streak, often being perceived as "obsessed" with their trade. These are traits that, when combined with high moral standing and intellectual honesty, augur well for investors.

Personal references, wherever possible, are a key part of the investment decision-making process. We often joke that the due diligence process should go all the way back to kindergarten! (Well, half joke). The more information regarding integrity that can be gleaned about a person, the better it is. After all, a good investor-manager relationship is a long-term partnership that should last many years.

Thoughtfulness is another trait that is necessary for any investment manager. Rash decision making is essentially guaranteed to yield disaster, so instituting a deliberate process for idea development is important for any company managing people's assets. Risks can develop in unprecedented ways and investment managers need to be proactive in assessing where threats to their clients' wealth may arise. Thoughtfulness also helps establish emotional stability, which is extremely important in an investment manager. When positions are well thought-out, rash decisions to the detriment of investors are much less likely.

Just as there are noteworthy characteristics that are necessary, there is one characteristic that is notably unnecessary: genius. Being *smart* is a baseline for any investment manager but being a *genius* is simply not necessary. History is littered with investment managers who, forgetting the importance of being not only smart but also thoughtful, had catastrophic results. The most well-known example of such catastrophe is that of Long-Term Capital Management (LTCM), which we discussed in Chapter Four.

Do the data support the manager?

Making sure that the information gathered from managers is corroborated by data is where "the rubber meets the road" in the selection process. Many investment managers will speak about their experience and consistency through varied market environments. Far fewer managers are able to back it up with their historical performance.

Thankfully, data on investment managers and the computer programs required to analyze that data are very accessible today. Almost all managers will provide prospective investors with data showing monthly returns and how they stack up against the no-fee comparable indices (like the S&P 500 or NASDAQ). There are several good software programs that allow investors to compare dozens of different managers on a head-to-head basis based on any number of criteria.

Many investors, however, read too much into the statistics on investment managers. Purely quantitative analysis devoid of thoughtful decision making yields undesired results. That being said, data are very useful for analyzing mass amounts of information and detecting situations where the numbers do not "agree" with the assertions of investment managers.

Are the third parties in the investment process capable and trustworthy?

There are many third parties that are deeply involved in the investment process (the investor and the investment manager being the first two parties). The three most important third parties are the broker, the administrator and the auditor.

Brokers

Brokers are responsible for the custodianship of assets and, in many cases, provide lending and research services to managers. In terms of custodianship, brokers are federally regulated entities in North America, so their assets are insured by their respective federal governments. All the major banks and many smaller institutions provide brokerage services. Unfortunately, even federally insured brokerage firms can fall victim to fraud. In 2011, for example, MF Global, one such brokerage firm, went into bankruptcy and revealed that client assets held under custodianship had been mishandled.[4] Frankly, there is very little one can do to avoid such a situation except to try to diversify across managers who use different brokers.

In terms of lending and research, it is very important that certain standards are met in the relationship between the manager and the brokers. Managers who borrow money, whether to sell securities short or to use leverage, need to have a good relationship with their brokers. Managers who borrow are subject to "margin calls," which occur when the brokerage firm demands that all capital be repaid, forcing managers to sell assets at inopportune (often the most inopportune) times. Ideally, managers who short-sell or use significant leverage in their investment process should utilize the services of more than one broker. Second, investors need to be wary of arrangements between managers and brokerage firms in the form of "soft dollars." Soft dollar arrangements occur when a manager directs business towards a certain brokerage firm in exchange for the brokerage firm providing services to the manager. Sometimes, the services provided to the manager have nothing to do with the investors (i.e. paying the operating costs of the manager) but the costs, often in the form of higher trading commissions, are borne directly by the investors. Ideally, soft dollar arrangements should be entirely avoided. In some cases, where soft dollars are unavoidable, investors must make sure that services provided to the manager from brokerage firms directly benefit the investors (i.e. improving investment research) rather than just the investment manager.

Administrators

Administrators are responsible for keeping track of all the assets under management. The administrator calculates the net asset value (NAV) of the fund and enforces rules and regulations for asset valuation. Even though many people are unaware of the administrator's role, it plays an integral role in the investment process. One stark example illustrating the importance of researching a manager's administrator was in the case of one of the largest investment frauds in history. Bernard Madoff, the hedge fund manager whose Ponzi scheme defrauded investors of tens of billions of dollars, was his own administrator. As a result, there was no one to provide a check against his alleged investment returns! Many "sophisticated" investors piled into Madoff's fund, forgoing due diligence on his administrator, and lost their invested capital as a result.

Auditors

Auditors provide an integral part of the investment process which is similar to that of administrators. The auditor will validate (or invalidate) the information provided by the administrator and provide a professional opinion on not only the investments but also the operations of the investment manager. Needless to say, auditors need to be reputable and capable. Auditing is often done by one of the "Big Four" accounting firms: KPMG, Deloitte, PricewaterhouseCoopers, Ernst & Young. In the case of Madoff, his auditor was a tiny, obscure accounting firm, in Rockland County, NY, handling a multi-billion dollar operation. Such types of arrangements are a red flag for prospective investors and should be investigated as a key component of the due diligence process.

Does the operating structure of the manager serve my best interests?

Issues with operating structure can have a significant effect on investment risk and returns. Central to the issue of the operating structure are fees. As an investor, clearly one always wants to minimize the fees. Of equal importance, and lesser notice for many investors, is that the fees charged must, to the greatest extent possible, align the interests of the investment manager with those of the investors.

Investment managers typically charge two types of fees simultaneously – management fees and incentive fees. Management fees are charged regardless of investment performance and can amount to anywhere from 0.2% to 4% of assets under management. Incentive fees are charged in proportion to the investment performance in any given year and can amount to anywhere from 10% to 25% of gains. **From the investor's standpoint, all other things being equal, it is better if the income earned by the investment manager depends much more on incentive fees than on management fees because only incentive fees are conditional on the investor actually earning money.** In general, investment managers that earn the lion's share of their income from incentive fees are, to a greater extent, putting their money on the line alongside investors.

There are two additional fee-related operating structures that are important to note. "High watermarks" and "hurdles" benefit investors by providing an additional alignment of interests through adjustments to fee terms. With a high watermark, the investment manager must make up for past losses before earning an incentive fee again. In the absence of a high watermark, the investment manager can still earn performance fees in a given year, despite losing clients' money over the long-term. High watermarks, therefore, align the long-term interests of the investment manager with those of the investors. Hurdles similarly affect the incentives of investment managers. Hurdles require that managers earn a return above some specified amount before earning any incentive fees. If a hurdle is 6%, for example, then a manager will not earn any incentive fees during a year in which it provides investors with a 5% return. The manager must not only provide gains to investors but also provide gains commensurate with the risk being undertaken.

In addition to fee-based operating structures, there are other operating structures that are very important. Investment managers often institute "gates" and "lockups"– conditions that prevent investors from redeeming their capital under certain circumstances. Such conditions restrict liquidity but provide stability, so they can be either a burden or a blessing to investors depending on the situation. Such terms need to be understood before investing and must align with the specific needs of the investor. For example, if an investor may need to redeem at some point in the near future, his or her needs will be different than those of another investor who is able to keep capital in one place for many years.

Operating structure issues extend beyond the fund terms and into the investment management company itself. Is the company employee-owned or owned by a large financial institution? Do the analysts and portfolio managers have a vested interest in the success of the company? Some investment managers require employees to reinvest a portion of their salary along with the investors. **Senior professionals should have the vast majority or the entirety of their personal net worth invested alongside their clients. This condition creates a situation in which the investment manager has "skin in the game." Its importance cannot be overestimated.** If a portfolio manager is unwilling to invest the vast majority of his or her own money along with their clients' money, then, frankly, their motivations are suspect or their confidence is lacking. In either case, it is a problem.

As time goes on, there are more interesting and compelling operating structures popping up everywhere. The investment management industry is increasingly competitive. This has resulted in increased purchasing power on the behalf of investors. One recent structure that is proliferating is one in which lower-level research analysts and traders, who are at the core of the investment process but often lack the capital to co-invest, are granted a "sub-advisor" track record based on their performance separate from the overall performance of the fund.

For a young analyst starting his or her career, garnering personal credit for making choices that benefit investors can provide a compelling springboard for future opportunities in the industry. Such non-monetary operating terms, in addition to a fee-based incentive alignment, can help create an operating structure that benefits investors in a meaningful and impactful way.

Is there enough communication and transparency to monitor the investment over time?

Communication between the investment manager and investors should be consistent, meaningful, and reliable. There *is* such a thing as too much information – as investment managers should never let the time-consuming communication process interfere with investment research – but clients need to be kept abreast of what is going on with their capital at least quarterly[5]. Such communication should be in plain English rather than professional jargon and should come from a reliable, senior professional at the investment management firm.

The reason for all this trouble is that, even after an investor has made the decision to invest, he or she needs to evaluate on a consistent basis whether to remain invested. Investors need to know if a manager is straying from the investment mandate or making careless decisions.

The extent to which investment managers are willing to discuss specific investments in a fund context varies across the industry. Some managers are very happy to discuss their investment holdings, whereas others guard their intellectual property like Fort Knox. In either case, managers should speak about what decisions they are making and why, even if they do not discuss specific investments. If an investor is not up to date with what is going on with a given investment manager, even in spite of fantastic investment returns, they should divest unless they are able to ascertain meaningful and reliable information.

How does the macroeconomic picture affect this investment?

Whereas the other questions on this checklist are generally underemphasized, this question is probably overemphasized. Unfortunately, predicting the future when it comes to the overall economy is exceptionally difficult, if not entirely impossible. Few people have been able to bet successfully based on general market trends over long time-horizons. Moreover, many investments are only related to the macro-economy in the short term rather than the long term, so overemphasis on macroeconomics can be distracting. That being said, macroeconomic expectations should be included in the investment process to the extent that they lead to sensible asset allocations.

From time to time, certain asset classes become so clearly over-valued that investors should reduce their exposure to them. For example, the U.S. stock market, always prone to booms and busts over history, had various stages at which lowering exposure would have been prudent. In December 1999, for example, the price-to-earnings multiple of the S&P 500 was over 40 times, meaning that, absent of growth, an investor would have to wait 40 years after investing before the earnings would accumulate to what they paid![6] In such a case, where a correction towards historical norms is highly likely, investors need to re-evaluate their positions and cover their exposures to risk.

Such decision making is much easier said than done. Using the late-nineties stock market example, a person would need a very strong sense of conviction and self-control to take money out of the equity markets, which had, for a decade, provided investors with such easy money. Taking money off the table or making the decision to not put additional money on the table can be a painful decision. This difficult process is done automatically when investors rebalance their portfolios to weights predetermined in an investment policy statement.

Ironically, the best macroeconomic indicators often come from trusted investment managers focused primarily on the microeconomics (i.e. the fundamentals of specific companies). For example, in his 1999 letter to Berkshire shareholders, Warren Buffet expressed his "expectation — indeed...the virtual certainty — that the S&P [would] do far less well in the [following] decade or two than it [had] done since 1982." This expectation was in advance of the "lost decade" in equities. Mr. Buffett did not predict any of the macroeconomic "shocks" that precipitated either of the two stock crashes from 2000 to 2010. Rather, he was simply unable to find companies valued at cheap enough market prices to be worthwhile investments, leading him to understand that the stock market was generally overvalued. If talented and experienced investment managers are unable to find good investments in their respective markets, then that is a strong indication their market is overvalued and due for a correction.

The Bottom Line

Extensive thought must be put into manager selection. Ultimately, an investor depends on investment managers to uphold their fiduciary duty, so finding capable and trustworthy managers is one of the most important parts of the investment process. Small differences in performance on a year-to-year basis add up over time and, as a result of compounding, have a dramatic effect on the appreciation of one's wealth. Since the vast majority of investment managers fail to earn higher returns than the passive indexes after fees, investors must be very selective.

There are many useful quantitative measures that investors can use to evaluate managers, but common sense alone can go a long way in manager selection. Sometimes, asking simple questions is the best way to get to the heart of the matter. Ultimately, a combination of quantitative and qualitative methods should be employed.

"There is no security on this earth; there is only opportunity."

- General Douglas MacArthur

Chapter Eight

The Death of the Insurance Dodo and Alternative Risk-Free Strategies

Having analyzed how we view manager selection, it is important to turn our attention to an example of an "alternative" asset, with a remarkably high return per unit of risk - life insurance.

In this chapter, we will use insurance as a case study for other creative investment options (and there are many of them), and explore why this, often bemoaned and somewhat distasteful asset, can be such a remarkable investment.

For starters, let us provide some context. Life insurance is in a state of flux in Canada and around the world. Canada's two largest life insurance companies (Sun Life and Manulife) have increased their rates by over 20% on certain types of insurance in the past year, and most other companies are following suit. One type of insurance that is particularly affected by this development is permanent life insurance, which could be largely stripped of its tremendous value, up to now, as a remarkable investment vehicle.

As investment consultants, we think of insurance in a very different way than the insurance broker industry does. We view insurance not as a product to be sold but rather one of many investment options which can be useful, given the right circumstances. In this sense, insurance can be considered as an alternative to risk-free bonds and other low-risk investments, and should be evaluated based on the same criteria – specifically, insurance should offer a high rate of return for a given amount of risk. In fact, permanent life insurance has been, from a return-per-unit-of-risk perspective, the best investment we have seen in over 15 years in the business of investment research. Unfortunately, this type of insurance is quickly disappearing from the marketplace, if it is not already a thing of the past.

What is Permanent Life Insurance and Why Should I Care?

In its basic form ("Term to 100"), permanent life insurance has (a) a policy which lasts for the entire life of the insured, (b) a fixed payout and (c) fixed periodic premiums. The payout and premiums are determined at the beginning of the policy. Permanent term to 100 insurance can be contrasted with "term insurance," which also provides coverage at a fixed rate of premium payment but only for a limited period of time (much like car or house insurance).

From an investment standpoint, permanent life insurance can be very valuable. It is a virtually risk-free investment which often has a higher after-tax return than other risk-free investments. Unlike the case with term insurance, the beneficiaries of a permanent insurance policy fully expect to receive a payout when the insured person dies. This is because the permanent insurance policy is designed to remain in force until that death. Term insurance, in contrast, is designed to lapse before the insured person dies due to rapidly increasing premiums as that expected death approaches. The reason for this certainty in regard to the safety of permanent insurance is the extremely high level of regulatory oversight in Canada, which ensures insurance companies' solvency vis-à-vis policy holders.[1]

Permanent life insurance can also have a cash value while the insured person is alive and, increasingly, a market value, should the owner of the policy wish to dispose of it. Such policies can be used as collateral for a loan or can be sold.[2] These characteristics are unique to permanent life insurance – they do not apply to term life insurance or other types of insurance.

The Death of the Insurance Dodo

Between the years of 2010 to 2012, not only did rates increase substantially for certain types of life insurance but entire policies ceased to be offered. Some of our nation's largest insurance companies took these measures under pressure to restore their profitability.

The most important investment vehicles for insurance companies to back up their permanent insurance policies (in order to have the funds available, if someone cashes out a policy) are long-term, low-risk fixed income investments. Sadly for insurance companies, interest rates have been steadily declining since the early 1980s and are now extremely low. Central Banks worldwide have indicated that they do not intend to raise rates in the near future. As a result, formerly profitable insurance policies, many of which were created and priced when interest rates were much higher, are now being either taken off the market or re-priced.

The diagram below shows the relationship between interest rates and insurance payouts. Over time, the payouts by insurance companies should mimic interest rates. Insurance companies need to make more money investing in fixed income vehicles than they expend on payouts to policyholders. Therefore, interest rate levels should keep payouts from being excessive while competition among insurance companies should keep payouts from getting too low.

The "payouts line" is reflected as jagged while the interest rate line looks straight because insurance companies are slower to change their premiums than fiscal authorities are to change interest rates.

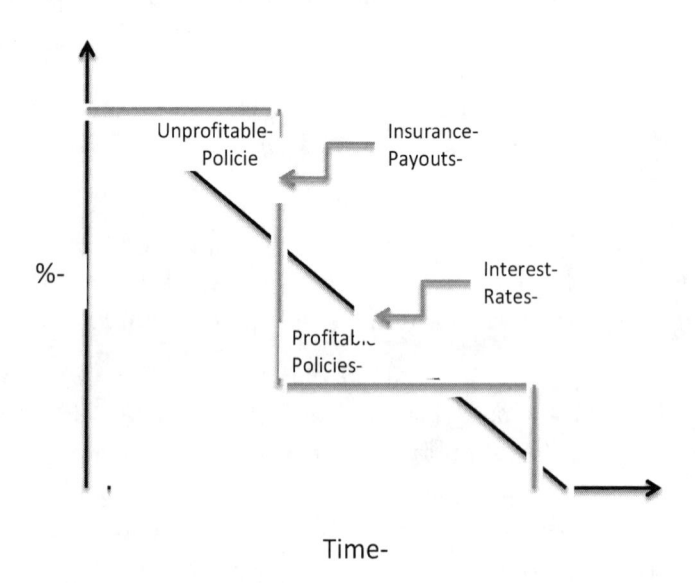

```
                    Unprofitable-      Insurance-
                    Policie            Payouts-

                                       Interest-
       %-                              Rates-

                    Profitable
                    Policies-


                            Time-
```

As a result, insurance companies tend to update the prices of their policies by making bigger premium adjustments, less frequently, rather than continuously. This explains the current state of flux; insurance companies have reached a tipping point and must take measures to stay afloat.

Although it is not certain that permanent life insurance policies will disappear completely, there will likely be additional pruning and re-pricing by insurance companies of the types of permanent life insurance that are most valuable to investors. These are the policies with the best "chassis" – the best core contracts and values driven by a low cost of insurance. Unfortunately, what usually happens when insurance companies eliminate policies is that the policies go the way of the Dodo Bird and never return.

The Insurance Chassis: Insurance as an Investment

Insurance in its basic form is very simple. If you are buying insurance, you are making a deal with an insurance company in which you pay them money either up front or over time in exchange for them paying your beneficiaries a larger lump sum at a future date dictated by the death of the insured person(s). There can be many bells and whistles attached to a policy but at heart it is a simple transaction. We like to call this simple, core part of the transaction the insurance "chassis."

In a car, the chassis is the structure which holds the wheels, body and engine together. Without a strong chassis, you are likely to end up with a pile of disparate junk rather than a functioning machine. In an insurance policy, the chassis is the minimum premium you pay and the amount your beneficiaries get out at the end.

If a person gets an insurance policy with a strong chassis that is then customized to their personal needs with additional provisions, the investment potential can be exceptional. Unfortunately, as insurance policies with strong chassis become extinct, opportunities to attain exceptional risk-adjusted returns will disappear. If insurance companies are providing guaranteed returns, to life expectancy, in the mid-to-high single-digit range, and making less than that lending out at current interest rates, how can they sustain this negative spread?

Insurance companies are extremely large institutions which have been around for decades. They can take a very long time to react to problems which are below their radar screens, and these strong-chassis permanent life insurance policies flew stealth for years. These life insurance policies were not always unprofitable for insurance companies. Until around 1990, you could get a 10% return on a term deposit in Canada. In 1982, the return on a 30-year Treasury bond was 14%! Back when interest rates were that high, insurance companies could afford to offer policies with exceptional returns.

As Canadian and worldwide interest rate practices changed, however, many of the old insurance policies continued to be offered in the marketplace, mostly due to inertia and the lower volumes at which such policies were sold. These lower selling volumes may have had something to do with lower compensation to agents selling these products. Although many insurance brokers have their clients' best interests at heart and act accordingly, the combination of the two adages that (a) "insurance is sold, not bought" and (b) "the best policy for the client is the worst for the broker" lead to a market in which, generally speaking, strong-chassis permanent life insurance policies are undersold and can remain in the marketplace despite being unprofitable.

Tax Benefits of Insurance

A discussion of insurance as an investment would not be complete without getting into the Canadian tax element of insurance. The investment return on a superior permanent life insurance policy is due in part to the strong-chassis element described above and in part to the favorable tax laws in Canada for life insurance policy holders.

Life insurance proceeds are one of only two tax-free "investment" receipts in Canada (the other is the proceeds from the sale of a primary residence). The gains on the investment – which is the payout by the insurance company minus the premiums paid by the policyholder – are provided to the beneficiaries without any tax having to be paid. Having said that, there is a 2% tax on all insurance premiums paid and deposits to life insurance policies.

In addition to the tax benefit on gains, there are additional tax benefits if one's corporation is the owner and beneficiary of the life insurance policy. These tax laws are somewhat technical but, in short, they can be used to significantly reduce tax expenses for shareholders vis-à-vis distributions from a corporation.[3]

Personally owned life insurance policies can also provide additional tax benefits. When a person dies and wealth is transferred to his or her children, any appreciation in the value of the assets is taxed as capital gains. These capital gains can be offset by donations after death and tax-free insurance death benefit proceeds are an ideal source of liquidity from which to make such donations. During the course of a person's life, there is a limit on the value of donations that can be deducted each year for tax purposes. In the last year of life, however, a person can deduct an unlimited amount of donations for tax purposes. If one were to give away enough money, he or she could wipe out all the taxes – capital gains and income – eligible in the year of death.

We have been able to show clients how, through investing in a strong chassis life insurance policy, they could eliminate taxes on death while still providing far more for their family and favorite cause(s). A person could buy a policy which leaves quite a bit for the family and quite a bit for charity, and get a tax break in the process which is particularly high as a result of the donation tax laws regarding the final year of life. How much better can it be?

The Bottom Line

As investment consultants, we are always seeking investment opportunities with more return per unit of risk. Over the past 15 years of investment experience, we have found many such opportunities in permanent life insurance policies. As an asset class, insurance can offer certain people tremendous upside with virtually no downside risk.

Besides using something as simple as insurance for an alternative investment strategy, the impetus for this chapter was to share information about permanent life insurance before imminent changes in the industry render the prospective returns mediocre relative to the values that policies have provided up to now. As the insurance world continues to undergo its state of flux, we expect strong-chassis permanent life insurance policies to continue to disappear as they are either taken out of the marketplace or re-priced upwards.

Every single policy which we recommended to our clients three, five, and ten years ago has since been eliminated or re-priced by insurance companies. Unfortunately, they were too good for the insurance companies to keep offering them. Today, there may still be a few opportunities for wealthy individuals and families to invest using permanent life insurance. Soon, however, we expect these opportunities to become as extinct as the Dodo Bird.

"It ain't what you don't know that gets you in trouble – it's what you know for sure that just ain't so."

- Mark Twain

Chapter Nine

Getting a Good Night's Sleep

Mastering the Psychology of Investing

We have just spent eight chapters discussing investment best practices. We reviewed numerous strategies to help you make wiser, safer, and more informed investment decisions, doing everything in your power to set yourself up for success. And, surprisingly, that's the easy part. The most difficult part is sticking to your plan, and protecting your estate from the only person that can completely sabotage even the best of plans: Yourself.

As Walt Kelly famously wrote in his 1970 Earth Day pogo comic, *"We have seen the enemy and he is us."* Humans are emotional creatures, who, even when following the best advice, can still lose sleep over their investments and make irreparable mistakes. Sure, having a trusted advisor, who is entirely in your corner, without any conflicts of interest, will help. However, we are still human.

It is fascinating to note that the word *human* is derived from Carl Linnaeus's 1758 work, *Systema Naturae*, where he coined the term *homosapiens*. Homosapien is a further derivation of the Latin words *homo*, meaning "earthly being," and *sapient*, meaning "wise." Amazingly, in the generations that followed, human became common parlance, and sapient petered out. Essentially we dropped the "wise," leaving us with just the "earthly being."

As "earthly beings" we make mistakes and things do not always proceed as we may have planned. Given this reality, we are, for the most part, control-seeking creatures. We clean our living spaces to feel in control of our surroundings, we watch what we eat (or, at least, try to) to control our bodily response, and keep track of our bills to control our expenditures. Just about all our activities are rooted in an attempt to control our environments, circumstances, or destiny. To control something, one must be able to understand it and have the capacity to manipulate it. If the object is beyond our capacity to understand or manipulate, there is simply no way to control and manage it. Ironically, however, recent research suggests that what we understand least is ourselves – our minds, bodies, and emotions, all of which impact our ability to make investment decisions.

Background

In recent years we have seen the emergence of a remarkable field of behavioral economics and, more specific to our conversation, behavioral finance. The primary difference between behavioral economics and traditional economics is the assumption that humans are rational and logical creatures. Traditional economists would build models on rational behaviors, while behavioral economists would argue that humans are only as logical as the biases that govern them.

Behavioral economists claim that our physiological and psychological make-ups leave us susceptible to self-deceptions, biases, mental gaps, and a host of other human failings that distort our judgment. In this chapter we have identified, what we believe to be, the nine most common susceptibilities and frailties in judgment, which play a role in our investment decisions[1]. For most of us, it is nearly impossible to completely avoid these biases, as they may be our initial reflexes. However, simply being aware of them, and reviewing them on a regular basis, will help you to make better investment decisions.

1. Jealousy Driven Decisions

> *"O beware, my Lord, of jealousy. 'Tis the green-eyed monster which mocks the meat it feeds on."*
>
> *- Shakespeare*

While greed certainly affects many, and can lead to poor decision making, especially when it involves taking excessive risks, there is no greater wealth killer than envy. Our desires and aspirations are driven more by coveting what we see around us than simply an arbitrary amassment of wealth. Besides the spending frenzy that envy can spur, looking over one's shoulder will invariably result in bad investment decisions.

Similarly, there is a common phenomenon psychologists refer to as herding, or the lemming effect, which simply means following the majority. This force is so deeply entrenched in our beings that historians and sociologists claim it is a survival instinct from millennia ago. They surmise that herding behavior was a crucial life-preservation tool when crisis struck, and those who survived tended to follow the flock, fleeing at the first signs of danger.

While herding may make sense when under siege, it never makes for good investment practice. It is unquestionably difficult to feel like you're standing on the sidelines while everyone around you is making money, or to be losing money and holding on to your positions while others seem to be heading for the exit. In fact, it is this very behavior that drives value investors, who are good at intelligently weathering a storm of panic and irrational sell-offs, to buy quality assets at irrationally cheap prices. Conversely, it is this very phenomenon that leads to the downfall of the unwitting lay investor (i.e. the masses).

Review the fundamentals of your investment decisions regularly. If they are intact, keep your head down, and ignore the world. The day will come when you will look back and be very glad that you did.

2. Misunderstanding Operating Incentives

"I have never seen a management consultant's report, in my long life, that didn't end with the following paragraph: 'What this situation really needs is more management consulting.'"

- Charles (Charlie) Munger

There is an incredible under-appreciation for the role that incentives play. Economists believe that incentives, especially financial and remunerative incentives, are the quiet driving force behind most of what we do. To illustrate this point, Charlie Munger often recounts the experience of Joseph Wilson, the founder of Xerox, which we see manifested in every corner of the business world. Wilson had introduced a much better, newer, and more cost-effective machine. Yet, he couldn't understand how this vastly superior machine was selling so poorly in relation to the older and inferior version. Of course, when he dug deeper he discovered that the compensation arrangement with the salesmen provided greater commissions on the inferior machine.

This is, of course, an old and common story. Incentives create what economists call 'agency costs.' In every professional relationship these added costs need to be very carefully identified at the outset. As we have stated in Chapter 2, "Product vs. Process," understanding what you are actually being sold should pre-empt any transaction.

In the world of financial services, there is no shortage of misnomers and mistitles deliberately designed to muddle what you are buying. Sales people will refer to themselves as "advisors" and "consultants." This behavior is not necessarily less common in the world at large. One of our colleagues had an experience, where he met a fellow at a dinner party, who introduced himself as a "nutrition consultant." Thinking that he could benefit from improving his diet, our colleague said that he would be happy to speak again. The "nutrition consultant" eagerly followed up and they arranged to meet. While the consultant took some measurements and asked our colleague to complete a health survey, it soon became clear that our "nutrition consultant" was nothing more than a salesman for Herbalife, selling two "solutions" (i.e. dietary shakes, which could only be purchased from him on a monthly basis) for every client. While this may be a common pitfall, the average investor is not sufficiently conscious of this danger to protect against it.

Incentives do not simply have to be compensatory or financial in nature. There is also a bias of reciprocation, for just about any good that was done. Dr. Robert Cialdini and Steve Martin[2] describe a famous study on the reciprocity bias. The study, known as the "Coca-Cola" experiment,[3] examined people who thought they were evaluating art. For each person, the experimenter's assistant (who appeared as just another participant), would leave the room at the same time. In some cases, he would return with a can of Coke, saying "I asked the experimenter if I could get myself a Coke, and he said it was okay, so I bought one for you, too." At the end of the experiment, this very same assistant asked the subjects if they would buy a 25-cent raffle ticket from him to help him win a prize. Those participants, who received a Coke from the assistant, bought twice as many raffle tickets as the ones who did not receive a Coke. Not only that, but they also paid far more than the value of the Coke.

Cialdini and Martin quote other research, such as an experiment that demonstrated how placing a couple of free mints with diners' bills increases tips by up to 23%[4]. Similarly, they show how the Hare Krishna achieved remarkable fundraising successes by giving all their prospects a free red flower prior to asking for a donation. The bottom line is that the reciprocity bias is almost always in play, making us considerably more generous and, at times, more concessionary than perhaps we should be.

In the sphere of investments, this can be particularly dramatic, as people often entrust enormous sums of money to professionals who have given them something relatively small, such as a bottle of scotch, box-seats at a home game, or a simple Christmas card. These are irrational decisions, but they have been in effect since time immemorial, and should be protected against when making investment decisions. It is for this reason that Sam Walton, the founder of Walmart, would not let a purchasing agent take a handkerchief or a pen from a salesman at the risk of losing his or her job. Walton wanted to avoid any whiff of reciprocity.

Simple and avoidable issues, like conflicts of interest, can actually be policed out of your business and your life. That is why we, at Prime Quadrant, obsess about how, by whom, and in what way a service provider is compensated. Conversely, in what ways are the clients making decisions based on reciprocity, rather than common sense?

Take a step back and reflect on what extent you would consider this investment if someone, about whom you are neutral, brought you the very same opportunity.

3. Fear Driven Decisions

> *"We must build dikes of courage to hold back the flood of fear."*
>
> - *Martin Luther King, Jr.*

In 1985, economists Rajnish Mehra and Edward C. Prescott coined the term Equity Premium Puzzle. In simple terms, the Equity Premium Puzzle highlights the fact that individuals will invest in bonds even though the historic returns of public equities are incomparably greater. These economists argue that the returns of equities are so much greater that it is almost irrational for the investment community to have as much exposure to bonds as it does. What the Equity Premium Puzzle suggests is that fear and the prospect of loss compel us to make overly-cautious decisions at the expense of substantially superior options.

This concept is certainly not new. It is the very basis of decision theory, first developed by Amos Tversky and Daniel Kahneman. Tversky and Kahneman's research suggests that, psychologically speaking, losses are almost twice as impactful on us as gains. A simple example of this is that someone who receives $100 will not gain nearly the measure of satisfaction that will be lost if one loses $100. Similarly, people are less excited about getting a 5% discount than they are upset about a 5% surcharge. That is also precisely why salespeople are dying for you to "try" their products. They are well aware that, even if you are not 100% thrilled with the product, once you are holding on to something, the bias of loss aversion will make it more difficult to part with.

In investment terms, since equities are far more prone to draw downs, investors will invariably overweigh their portfolios with bonds. The fear of losing money, as markets start to nosedive, has either one of two negative effects. First, people tend to sell as soon as the market moves in a negative direction. This is a losing strategy, which will slowly eat away at your capital base. Second, people tend to not sell when they should. Often, when the fundamentals have changed, it is better to cut bait and move on. However, many will fall for the sunk cost fallacy[5], where past expenses are weighing in on decisions about your future.

To counteract this bias, Dr. Shlomo Benartzi, a professor at the UCLA Anderson School of Management, suggests that clients adopt a Ulysses Strategy, with their financial advisors (and vice versa), in dealing with market movements.

At the heart of the Ulysses mythology are the Sirenuse Islands. According to lore, these islands were renowned for their melodic Sirens, whose tunes and songs were so irresistibly captivating that seamen would instantly and irrationally jump into the sea upon hear them, in a mad dash to approach the shores (where they would be killed). As the story goes, none of those that ventured towards the sounds ever survived, so no living person knew the true essence of the Sirenuse songs.

Ulysses was determined to be the first to hear the songs and survive. He told his crew to fill their ears with beeswax to block out the sound and asked to be tied to the ship's mast. He commanded the crew to ignore any of his cries or pleas, should he ask to be released. Despite going temporarily insane, screaming and struggling with all his might to break free, Ulysses overcame the temptation to rashly and foolishly swim towards the islands.

Investors (and especially their investment advisors) would, from time to time, do themselves a favour by putting wax in their ears, and ignoring the music of the market. In a relationship between a psychiatrist and patient, there are occasional Ulysses contracts employed. This is a legal arrangement, where both parties have agreed to override a present or future request in favor of a past request made by that patient[6]. Similar arrangements need to be made between investors and their advisors, determined by pre-agreed upon jumps or tumbles in the market. This allows investors to combat the emotional turmoil brought on by loss aversion, and avoid the sunk cost fallacy.

To help you prevail through your times of uncertainty and fear, you should ensure that you have an agreement with your advisor that resembles a Ulysses contract.

4. Illusion of Control

> *"Man does not control his own fate.*
> *(The women in his life do that for him.)"*
>
> *- Groucho Marx*

While teaching at Harvard, the legendary behavioral psychologist, Burrhus Frederic ("B.F.") Skinner, developed a conditioning chamber, often referred to as the "Skinner box."[7] This box revealed a remarkable human flaw of being tempted by unpredictable results (which, to some extent, also suggests that we are hard-wired for gambling). Skinner discovered that of all forms of reinforcement, variable schedule reinforcement[8], which offers an incentive after an unpredictable number of prompts, results in one of the highest rates of response. In other words, if we don't know that pulling a lever will produce a result on that particular pull (but we know that sometimes it will) we are likely to pull that lever for longer than if we knew it produced a positive result in some consistent rhythm. This is particularly troubling, as it means that we have a bias towards gambling, where the probability of a payoff is lower than the stakes themselves.

Why then do we do it, if not for an illusion (and delusion) of control? As we mentioned earlier, humans are control-seeking creatures, and would only love to believe that we have the control we crave. Our minds cannot help but wander to that happy place, where our control over our environment is exaggerated.

How exactly are we fooled into this? Research suggests that when people are given a trivial choice, they exaggerate the extent to which they can control the non-trivial matter[9]. So, between buying a lottery number picked by a machine and a lottery number that is picked by you, the hand-selected lottery will always yield greater sales, and carry with it greater conviction in the probability of success. While people do lose considerable amounts "playing the slots," in the aggregate, it doesn't compare to what is lost in blackjack or poker, where small decisions create a much greater illusion of control.

Allowing us to make small, and even irrelevant, decisions confounds our sense of control. This, of course, leads us to the next vulnerability, an irrational and exaggerated sense of self-confidence.

Before making an investment, consider and question to what extent an opportunity is subject to matters beyond your control.

5. Overconfidence

> *"To the man with a hammer, every problem tends to look pretty much like a nail."*
>
> *- Abraham Maslow*

There are interesting studies that demonstrate that approximately 90% of drivers believe that they are "better than the average driver,"[10] 68% of lawyers in civil cases believe their side will prevail, and 81% of new business owners think their business will succeed, but only 39% of their competition will even come close.

The research tells us that there is a natural tendency to overestimate one's ability. Similarly, as investors, we like to believe that we understand everything about the market and that we sit comfortably in the top quartile of investors.

Many do-it-yourself investors believe that by nimbly jumping in and out of stocks, they can beat the market. While this is not the topic of our chapter, as we have already mentioned in previous chapters, our experience and research suggests that market timing is incredibly risky and rarely works. The Dalbar report[11] on investor behavior continues to show that individual investors are not realizing anywhere near market rates of return in stocks and bonds because of frequent switching among "hot" stocks and trying to time the market.

The difficulty with overconfidence is that we tend to have limited attribution capacities, often pegging the success or failure of something on just a couple of variables.

In his book, *Thinking Fast and Slow*, Nobel Prize winner Daniel Kahneman describes how our brains suffer from overconfidence. This is not so much arrogance – though for some people that may be a part of it – as it is our tendency to believe past behaviour to be much more reliable as a predictive factor than we should, and to construct narratives to explain complex phenomena like the stock market, even though there are far too many variables affecting a particular stock's behaviour for us to really account for.

Within the bias of overconfidence, there are several mental vices in play. These include *over-optimism*, the tendency to perceive the future prospects of a venture more optimistically than historical evidence would warrant. *Selective memory* is yet another classic bias, whereby past experiences that may offer empirical insight for the current situation can be wholly ignored, since they don't conform to the desired result. These can all be subsumed into what psychologists refer to as the *confirmation bias*, which is the propensity of people to agree more with positive, rather than negative, statements about themselves. Research suggests that, subconsciously, the mind has a tendency to focus on the optimistic. Yet, consciously, it has a tendency to focus on the negative. Ultimately, not being aware of these biases will lead to bad investment decisions.[12]

Before any investment decision, simply ask yourself, "Am I overestimating my knowledge or understanding of this space? Is it possible that I am being too optimistic? What variables am I not considering?"

6. Social Proof

> *"Whenever you find yourself on the side of the majority, it is time to pause and reflect."*
>
> *- Mark Twain*

The bias we are probably most easily susceptible to is social proof, which essentially means drawing conclusions from the actions of others, amidst uncertainty and stress. In almost every social psychology program, the case of Kitty Genovese[13] has been used to demonstrate just how dramatic social proof is.

In the sphere of investing, the notion of social proof is, in some ways, contrary to the efficient market hypothesis. It has been outlined in Chapter Three that, in the aggregate, we do not always make rational decisions. Rather, we look to see what the people around us are doing. Since the majority of people are not great investors, the crowd will likely be a poor point of reference.

More danger emerges when the social proof comes from social sources that are intentionally misleading. In recent years, there has been a proliferation of fraudulent stock market practices, such as "pump and dump" schemes. In these duplicitous enterprises, penny stock promoters artificially inflate the price of a stock through false and/or misleading statements. Once the masses bite the bait, and the stocks run up in price, the operators of the scheme "dump" their overvalued shares. Consequently, the price falls back to (or below) its real value and investors are left holding the bag. By creating the aura of social proof through email newsletters, online bulletin boards and chat rooms, the penny-stock promoters establish inherent credibility and prey on the investing ignorance of the masses.

To mitigate the risk of social proof, one should ask themselves, "If I was the only one investing in this opportunity, would I still be happy to proceed?" This will force you to focus on what matters most, the fundamentals, and will result in better investment decisions.

7. Anchoring

In front of a large auditorium at MIT's Sloan School of Management, Professor Dan Ariely asked all the students in the room to write down the last two digits of their Social Security numbers. Subsequently, he asked them to place bids on various items, such as bottles of wine and boxes of chocolate. When the results were tallied, it was discovered that the group with higher two-digit numbers bid between 60-120% higher on the exact same items[14].

Countless studies of psychological research suggest that we are remarkably influenced by irrelevant information around us. This phenomenon, where simply seeing a random large number can influence a purchasing decision, is the basis of anchoring.

In behavioral economics, anchoring refers to our fixation on the price we paid for an item, regardless of its intrinsic worth or the relevance of that price today. We tend to latch on to what we paid, even after the facts have changed. Studies show that it's hard for our brains to let go when we have already invested time or a specific amount of money in an investment, no matter how much the price declines.

In addition to the price paid, there is also a form of generational anchoring that is often ignored. This anchor is set by witnessing where dramatic sums of money were made or lost. For example, despite the impact of the dot-com crash, the explosion of young millionaires in the dot-com era has shaped the thinking of a generation of investors. Similarly, those whose impressionable early years of investing were highlighted by the golden age of the stock market[15] are much more inclined towards stocks than the generation of the Depression era[16].

The best way to mitigate anchoring is to simply avoid making decisions on the fly. Weigh out your options in different places and contexts, to avoid being anchored by anything in your immediate environment. Discuss with someone older or younger than you are, and try to ignore the previous price you paid (or what someone else was willing to pay) for the asset.

8. Poor Human Calculators

"Mathematics is well and good but nature keeps dragging us around by the nose."

- Albert Einstein

We like to believe that we are fairly good at sizing up the world around us, which involves estimating and assessing probabilities. In reality, the human brain is actually quite poor in gauging probabilities. Time and time again, we miscalculate how large something may be, how long it will take and how much resources it will need. Partly, this is due to our biases towards overconfidence and over-optimism. However, there is also an element of simply not being wired for precision.

In a 1994 study, graduate students studying psychology were asked to estimate how many days it would take them to complete their theses. The average guess was 33.9 days. They also provided a best-case scenario (27.4 days) and a worst-case scenario (48.6 days). After all was said and done, the average completion period was 55.5 days, with less than 30% of the students completing their thesis in the predicted time period[17].

Research suggests that what we are usually doing is employing some crude heuristic, and are often misled by mere contrast, available information, overconfidence, and/or over-optimism.

Contrast is yet another mental trap, as the disparity between diametrically opposed sensations distorts and obscures our perceptions of reality. Dr. Robert Cialdini demonstrated this with his famous water bucket experiment[18], where the extent to which water was perceived to be hot or cold was most correlated with the temperature of the water that was touched beforehand.[19] People are over-influenced by contrast. We do not have an absolute scale, and contrast is often the best available heuristic. What this means is that we are easily susceptible to manipulation. (Thus, sales people will always offer the more expensive option first, as it makes the second option that much more palatable).

This inability to formulate an objective scale for every situation leaves us vulnerable to yet another bias, often referred to as the framing effect.

There is a famous Jewish story[20] about a man who was a smoking addict and approached his Rabbi, asking if he is allowed to smoke while praying to God. The Rabbi frowned, with a look of disapproval, and responded that it would be highly inappropriate. Somewhat disappointed, as the man walked away he came across another Jewish man, holding a prayer book and appearing to smoke and pray. Surprised and curious, he approached the fellow and asked him, "Sir, how is it that you're allowed to do this? The Rabbi forbade me from smoking as I pray." "Why simple," the young fellow responded, "I told him that I'm a regular smoker, and simply asked if it was okay to pray as I smoke."

Framing and contrast is the reason why we may go to great lengths to buy a $200 item at a $100 discount, but would not exert nearly the same effort in buying a $200,000 item with a $100 discount. Despite the fact that savings are the same, the contrast and frame makes the extra effort seem petty, and we'll say things like, "Once I'm spending that much money already, what difference does it make?"

Framing doesn't just impact small, irrelevant pricing decisions. Even life and death decisions can also be determined by how a response is framed. There is a famous study, often quoted by professors Dan Ariely and Daniel Kahneman, among others, in the field of medicine. In summary, two separate groups of doctors are presented with exactly the same medical condition. Both groups of doctors are then told that there is a new treatment available, which can cure the condition, and warned of the risks involved. However, the first group of doctors is told that there is a 5% mortality rate, while the second group of doctors is told that there is a 95% survival rate. Not surprisingly, the doctors for whom the high survival rate was referenced were considerably more supportive of the treatment than the doctors for whom the mortality rate was emphasized[21].

These biases are ever so present in the investment world. We're guilty of framing when we look at investment managers favourably when they outperformed an index that **they** themselves selected. A much better analysis would have been a comparison to their peers and all the alternatives in the markets.

Similarly, in the sphere of real estate development, private equity, and especially venture capital, we tend to grossly underestimate the amount of time (and resources) a venture will take.

The best solution for avoiding the miscalculation of framing bias is to not rush any decision. Shop around. Consult with your trusted advisors. There will always be another investment bus, so don't rush to get on one where you may not enjoy the ride.

9. Authority

> *"In the last analysis, every profession is a conspiracy against the laity."*
>
> *- George Bernard Shaw*

Quite possibly the most dangerous of all biases involves mindlessly obeying authority. Human beings seem to have built-in mechanisms that allow for the over-influence of, and respect for, authority figures. Respect for authority certainly has its place, but we have to first acknowledge its grip on our decision-making process and, most importantly, recognize its limits.

In 1961, during the trial of Nazi war criminal Adolf Eichmann, Yale University psychologist Stanley Milgram, decided to measure the extent to which individuals like Eichmann were aligned with Hitler's goals and motivations for the Holocaust. He wanted to determine whether there was either a common desire to commit genocide among those in the Nazi regime or merely such extensive authoritative pressure that perpetrators over-rode their personal moral beliefs.

Milgram recruited a wide variety of subjects and told them they would be studying the effect of punishment on learning ability. The experiment was set up so that all subjects ended up playing the "teacher." The "learner" was a hired actor. The "teachers" were asked to administer electric shocks to "learners," with increasing intensity, if questions were answered incorrectly. Unbeknownst to the teachers, the electric shocks were fake.

Shock levels, ranging from 15 to 450 volts were labeled, with dramatic emphasis on the higher shock levels (signs like "Danger: Severe Shock," and, past that, "XXX."). As the voltage was increased, the actors began to grunt, then to complain, then to beg to be released, and, ultimately, to scream in pain. If a "teacher" hesitated to inflict the shocks, the experimenter would pressure him or her to proceed, with statements such as "the experiment requires that you continue."[22]

In the end, while some participants dropped out of the experiment in the early stages, a *shocking* 65% of them were willing to apply the highest voltage level on the "learners." While many participants were disturbed administering the shock treatment, they subjected themselves to the authority of the experimenter.

As much as we would like to believe that Milgram's findings are exaggerated or aberrational, countless other studies corroborate them on the influence of authority. In research on junior co-pilots, it was found that approximately 25% of simulated flights crashed because the first officers failed to take control.[23] Similar research suggests that, in at least one-fourth of all cases, younger co-pilots will not contradict a senior pilot, even when they have the appropriate training and know that the plane is about to crash. They will defer to the authority of the senior pilot[24].

Over 1,600 psychological papers have been written on the Milgram experiment. Much less ink has been spent on the application of this research. Since people are typically not great at distinguishing between true experts and those who are just fancy-talking salespeople, submission to authority will rarely result in a winning strategy.

Avoiding the bias of authority is much more difficult than it may seem, especially because there is yet another factor in play. In social psychology, there is an often referenced concept of role theory. In short, role theory suggests that people tend to act in the way that other people would expect them to act.

In 1971, Stanford University's Dr. Philip Zimbardo conducted the famous Stanford Prison Experiment.[25] Zimbardo randomly assigned subjects to play the roles of "prisoners" or "guards." The "guards" were given sticks and sunglasses, while the "prisoners" were forced to wear chains and prison garments. They were all placed in the basement of the Stanford psychology department, which had been converted into a makeshift jail. As the experiment progressed, the guards became progressively more sadistic, neglecting the fact that the "prisoners" were not criminals, but simply their peers. Ultimately, a riot broke out, one of the prisoners became very ill (because he discovered that his "parole" was rejected), and after just six days the experiment was shut down for fear of the subjects' safety.

The Milgram and Zimbardo experiments demonstrate just how much influence authority can have over our decision-making process. In investing, our predispositions are particularly destructive when the traditional establishment of financial services deals in an exploitive manner with people who are not familiar with the field, such as the elderly and those who lack formal education. In industries where there is asymmetrical information and the lay community is reliant on the expertise of those selling solutions, "trust me" become the two most dangerous words in the English language.

With the proliferation of online resources and information, the trend of submitting to authority is starting to shift. People are beginning to challenge their doctors, lawyers, accountants, and investment managers. Salespeople cannot pull the wool over people's eyes as easily as they could in the past. However, the bias for authority still exists, and needs to be protected against.

To manage these biases and limit their negative influence, especially when it comes to your investments, it is important to remember that no one (regardless of their level of expertise) possesses a crystal ball. Accordingly, no one should be making important decisions without your firm understanding of the ramifications of those decisions. Whether in reference to your health, your children, your investment portfolio, or anything else, leaving it to the "experts" can have catastrophic results.

The Other Side of the Coin and Helpful Tips

It is important to point out that, while we need to be conscious of these various biases and mental menaces, there are also many benefits to all these biases and heuristics. If they did not exist, we would spend considerably more time on every exercise and activity, as the conscious mind would be unable to cope with every feasible calculation necessary to avoid these pitfalls. As the British economist John Maynard Keynes once said, "It is better to be roughly right than precisely wrong."

Besides the strategies we have already suggested, there are a number of tactical solutions for avoiding the problems these biases can lead to. One solution was a strategy employed by Carl Braun, a prominent American businessman who started the Braun Company, designing and constructing top-notch gas processing plants and oil refineries. Braun had a simple rule for all his communications. Every memo or discussion had to include the "Five W's" – Who, What, When, Where, and Why. Anyone who did not provide these five W's in any communication would get fired. Because of the complexity and dangers involved in building oil refineries, with small mistakes being potentially catastrophic, Braun was unforgiving about it. Braun knew that providing people with a context and a reason facilitated dialogue and constructive feedback. Employing this simple discipline in our investing decisions would go a long way.

Another concept, most famously championed by the Harvard Business School, is the use of decision trees. Decision trees help chart out all possible outcomes, and weigh the cost versus the benefit of proceeding in any specific direction. Other solutions can be as simple as preparing a checklist of all the possible biases, and trying to objectively review them before making any investment decision.

Most importantly, take ownership. Do not relegate your role and responsibility as the steward of your wealth. You have worked so hard to achieve it; why lose or abandon it now? Take the time, educate yourself, and when you feel comfortable, dip your toe in the water. There is no need to rush. The cash should not burn a hole in your pocket. You will make mistakes along the way, just as anyone will. In any case, don't just find a babysitter for your money, and expect it to be raised the way you would want it to be.

This suggestion does not preclude one from getting proper counsel from an investment professional. To the contrary, it would be imprudent not to. However, as we have mentioned throughout this book, assure that you have a trusted partner or advisor, who is purely and entirely an advisor, without any products to sell you or assets of yours to hold. Ensure that they help you develop your investment constitution, and live by it. Through this process, you will be equipped to circumvent these predispositions, get a better night's sleep, and, of course, make better investment decisions.

The Bottom Line

One should be conscious of the many factors that come into play when making investment decisions. Besides those already mentioned, there are many others. The nine mentioned in this chapter are, in our opinion, the most pernicious and ubiquitous of all. To recap:

1. Jealousy driven decisions may prompt us to look over our shoulders, when we should be keeping our heads down, and staying true to our convictions.
2. Miscalculating the influence of incentives may allow us to imbed potentially toxic conflicts of interest within the management structure of our investments.
3. Fear driven decisions may cause us to forfeit long-term success, at the expense of short-term anxiety.
4. Illusion of control may lead us to believe that the success of our investments is entirely in our hands.
5. Overconfidence results in an overly optimistic assessment of one's own ability.
6. Social proof may compel us take assurance in the actions of peers, rather than our convictions.
7. Anchoring may allow us to make poor quantitative decisions based on an arbitrary, possibly even misleading, benchmark or comparison.
8. Our poor human calculators cause us to misjudge important considerations.
9. Authority may deceive us into submitting to perspectives and stances that will not serve our purpose.

While these may seem overwhelming, with a healthy investment process and a properly incentivized trusted advisor, these biases can be systematically overcome. As we have said throughout the book, with these two resources in hand, coupled with the insights gleaned in the foregoing pages, you will avoid many costly mistakes and ultimately make better investment decisions.

Appendix A

Calculating the *return* on a portfolio is relatively simple. Since a portfolio is just a collection of assets, all one needs to do is take the average return of the assets that make up the portfolio. This average has to be weighted according to the assets' proportions in the portfolio. (For example, if an asset comprises 90% of a portfolio, it has nine times the effect on the portfolio returns as an asset that comprises only 10%.)

If we were to measure the return of a portfolio composed of two assets, Asset A and Asset B, we would use the following formula:

$$R_p = w_A \times R_A + w_B \times R_B$$

Where:

- w_A is the weight (proportion) of Asset A in the overall portfolio;
- R_A is the return on Asset A;
- w_B is the weight of Asset B in the overall portfolio; and
- And R_B is the return on Asset B.

If you can get past the symbols for a moment, the equation says something pretty straightforward: The return of an investment portfolio is equal to the weighted average returns of the underlying assets.

Understanding how the *volatility* of a portfolio is calculated requires a little more thought. Volatility is based on a measurement that you may not be familiar with: correlation. Correlation refers to how returns move in relation to one another, in terms of the direction and the degree of intensity. If assets A and B behave similarly under similar market conditions, then the two assets are said to be positively correlated. If they behave differently under similar market conditions, then the assets are negatively correlated.

If we were to measure the volatility of a portfolio composed of the same two assets, we would use the following formula:

$$\sigma_P^2 = w_A^2 \sigma_A^2 + w_B^2 \sigma_B^2 + 2 \times w_A w_B \sigma_A \sigma_B \rho_{A,B}$$

Where:

- is the weight (proportion) of Asset A in the overall portfolio;
- $_A$ is the volatility of Asset A;
- is the weight of Asset B in the overall portfolio;
- $_B$ is the volatility of Asset B;
- And , is the correlation between Asset A and Asset B. Correlation will always be greater than -1 and less than +1.

This equation essentially says that the volatility in a portfolio will depend on three things: the weights of the assets, the respective volatilities of those assets and the correlation between the assets.

Pretend for a moment that the third term (the part of the equation that reads $+2 \times w_A w_B \sigma_A \sigma_B \rho_{A,B}$) did not exist. The equation would just say that the volatility of an investment portfolio is equal to the weighted average of the volatilities in the underlying assets. It would just be the same calculation that we used earlier for the return of a portfolio. This third term, however, is very important: it contains the secret to diversification's "free lunch," which, as we wrote in Chapter Five, allows investors to get a disproportionately high decrease in volatility for a small decrease in expected returns.

The smaller $2 \times w_A w_B \sigma_A \sigma_B \rho_{A,B}$ is, the less volatility there will be. There are three ways this can be done: we can change the weights in the portfolio (change w_A and w_B), choose assets with lower volatilities (change σ_A and σ_B) or choose assets with lower correlations (change $\rho_{A,B}$). We might not want to change the weights of the assets, because that would affect our returns. We might also want to avoid lowering the volatility of the underlying assets because, as we mention many times in the book, assets with lower volatility often have lower returns. However, if we choose assets with lower correlations, we can decrease volatility without materially affecting our returns.

This relationship can also be illustrated in an example.

Let's say that we are constructing a portfolio of two assets, split 50-50 between Asset A and Asset B. Asset A has a return of 12% with 6% volatility. Asset B has a return of 8% with 4% volatility.

A portfolio that has allocated half of its funds to Asset A and half of its funds to Asset B is expected to return 10%. Remember, the return on the portfolio is just the weighted average return of the underlying assets. Meanwhile, the volatility of this portfolio will depend on the correlation between Asset A and Asset B. If the returns are strongly correlated, say at a level of .8, the portfolio's expected volatility will be:

$$\sigma_P^2 = w_A^2 \sigma_A^2 + w_B^2 \sigma_B^2 + 2 \times w_A w_B \sigma_A \sigma_B \rho_{A,B}$$

$$\sigma_P^2 = 0.5_A^2 0.06_A^2 + 0.5_B^2 0.04_B^2 + 2 \times .0.5_A 0.5_B 0.06_A 0.04_B (0.8)$$

$$\sigma_P = 4.75\%$$

On the other hand, if the returns are weakly correlated, say at a level of .01, the portfolio's expected volatility will be:

$$\sigma_P^2 = 0.5_A^2 0.06_A^2 + 0.5_B^2 0.04_B^2 + 2 \times 0.5_A 0.5_B 0.06_A 0.04_B (0.01)$$

$$\sigma_P = 3.62\%$$

Amazingly, this decrease in the portfolio volatility does not change the portfolio's expected return of 10%.

The Only Free Lunch in Finance

So long as a portfolio contains assets that are not perfectly positively correlated, the effects of diversification result in a lower portfolio volatility than each individual asset's volatility would suggest. Following along the same intuition, a low correlation between the returns within a portfolio of securities would imply a higher level of diversification. The more dissimilar the return patterns, the greater the volatility reductions.

Appendix B

In order to create a well-diversified portfolio, an investor should have return streams deriving value from different sources. Absolute return products are an important source of these returns. Hedge funds are a common vehicle employed to achieve absolute returns, as their structures allow fund managers wide discretion in the strategies they choose to follow and the investment products they use in order to exploit market inefficiencies (mispricing of marketable securities).

This discretion allows a manager to achieve consistent returns that are not related to the direction of the market, offering an interesting risk-reward proposition and an excellent diversification tool. The act of "hedging" allows some managers to isolate the specific risks and returns that they wish to be exposed to. Therefore, if hedged appropriately, a fund can be "neutral" to the forces of a market (the ups and downs of stock and bond markets), and derive all of its value from a manager's trading strategy. Hedge fund managers often exhibit an edge over ordinary market participants, as they function in less efficient markets – markets that require an expertise in a niche area – therefore creating returns that are inaccessible to most investors.

Absolute return strategies vary widely and can be founded on just about anything. For instance, there are hedge funds that implement algorithmic trading strategies to capitalize on changes in weather patterns. There was even a fund that monitored "tweets" in order to capitalize and apply trades based on global sentiment. Of course, we do not recommend such strategies (at least if you want to make money) but the point is that absolute return strategies offer investors an array of non-Traditional investment options.

Below, we will discuss four broad classes of strategies that are employed in order to achieve absolute returns: Event-Driven, Value-Driven, Quantitative Trend-Following, and Global Macro.

Event-Driven

Event-Driven strategies are exactly what they sound like – strategies that opportunistically invest based on special events that drive price movements of securities. Typically, the opportunity to buy a mispriced asset arises as a result of a complex corporate finance event, such as a bankruptcy or merger. A certain level of expertise is required in order to accurately analyze the event's implications on a security, which may ward off investors that are not knowledgeable on the subject. A fund manager generally completes each investment position within one year, which is a relatively short amount of time compared to other strategies. Although event-driven strategies do not completely avoid broader market forces, the value is derived from a different enough source to provide meaningful diversification, particularly over longer time horizons. Event-Driven strategies include, but are not limited to, Merger (or Risk) Arbitrage and Distressed Investing.

Merger Arbitrage is a trading strategy that revolves around the analysis of an expected takeover of one company – the target company – by another company – the acquiring company. A typical trade would involve selling short the stock of an acquring company while buying the stock of the target company. (Even after a merger is announced, a target company's shares typically trade at a lower price than the acquiring company's shares because there is uncertainty that the merger will be executed. If the merger goes through, then the shares will converge in price). This trade is essentially betting on the likelihood of the announced transaction actually closing, isolating the risk of the trade to the deal rather than the market.

Creating value through such trades depends on the manager's ability to define and assess all of the relevant factors that could affect the deal. For instance, the manager should understand the financing behind the merger, the sentiment of the target company with regards to being acquired and the relevent regulatory issues, among other factors.

Distressed Investing involves a fund manager taking a position in the securities (debt or equity) of a company undergoing financial difficulties and involved in a reorganization process – be it a restructuring, a recapitalization, or a bankruptcy. These securities are often trading at very depressed prices resulting from selling pressures of investors unable or unwilling to hold the securities of a company in such a state. The depressed prices can offer an opportunistic entry point for a manager who is capable of understanding the complex situation, and believes that the assets will recover to healthier valuations. The ability of an investor to value the securities and timing of the company's reemergence from the reorganization can yield superior returns. The broad market plays little role in determining this strategy's returns.

Value-Driven

Value-Driven investing is based on the very intuitive thesis of "buy low, sell high." To implement this strategy, a manager compares the market price of a security to its intrinsic value – its fair value based on a thorough understanding of the company. The success of this strategy is dependent on a manager's ability to identify undervalued and overvalued securities. An undervalued security is one that is selling in the market below its intrinsic value and an overvalued security is one that is selling in the market above its intrinsic value. Implementing the strategy involves taking long positions (buying) undervalued securities and taking short positions (selling) overvalued securities. Managers rely on changing company fundamentals or increasing market awareness to drive market prices of a securities towards their intrinsic values.

A security may be mispriced for many reasons. For example, perhaps the industry in which a company functions has been receiving a lot of positive or negative attention, driving a security's price above or below its fair value. A manager will take a position in a security hoping that, in due time, the security's market price will revert to its true value. A portfolio with equal amounts of long and short positions will not be exposed to market forces, but will derive its returns entirely from a manager's security selection. Returns will not be dependent on the direction of the overall market.

Quantitative Trend-Following

The Quantitative Trend-Following strategy allocates assets to capitalize on short-, medium- and long-term market movements, or "trends." The strategy is founded upon the premise that directional trends, driven by human biases, are persistent in all liquid markets. If price trends can be identified, trades can be implemented to generate returns, regardless of the direction of the market. Quantitative funds typically use algorithmic models to identify trend directions and systematically (based on pre-defined rules) decide the timing and size of each trade. These algorithms are designed using advanced statistical techniques and economic theory.

Although the mechanics behind the strategy are quite sophisticated, the intuition is rather straightforward: When there is an upward trend in an asset, take a long position, and when there is a downward trend in an asset, take a short position. The use of advanced algorithms and trading tools allows a fund to analyze broad sets of data across many markets, and trade a diverse portfolio across various asset classes in order to capture prevailing trends in a diversified and time-efficient manner.

Since Quantitative Trend-Following funds function across many markets and asset classes, and may go long or short in each, they exhibit a very low correlation to broad markets as compared to other strategies.

Global Macro

Absolute Return funds utilizing a Global Macro strategy analyze, forecast, and decide the market implications of macroeconomic and geopolitical developments. Returns are based on an investment manager's ability to make reasoned judgments about many interconnected and ever-changing puzzle pieces.

A manager will likely forecast interest rate trends, inflation, exchange rates, shifts in global economies, monetary flows and balances, and much more, in order to evaluate attractive markets and trading ideas. The Global Macro strategy employs the widest mandate and uses the broadest scope of investment instruments. Fund managers in this strategy are either going to make directional trades, betting on price movements, or make relative value trades, pairing long and short positions to exploit pricing discrepancies between instruments that should be similarly priced. It is common for managers of this strategy to take leveraged bets due to the nature of the investment instruments and trades involved. Over time, by alternating between views on macro conditions, these funds' returns should be independent of overall market returns.

Endnotes

Chapter 1

[1] In finance theory, the degree to which investments will behave similarly to one another is described by their "correlation". If two investments correlate highly with one another, it means that they will change in value similarly as events unfold. If two investments have low or negative correlations, it means that they will react differently as events unfold.

[2] Some of these risk-adjusted return measurements are the Sharpe Ratio, Jensen's Alpha, and the Treynor Ratio.

Chapter 2

[1] Who is not a passive "customer" in the traditional sense.

[2] Wessel, Robert. "Canadian Banks: The End of an Era" presentation, April 2012.

[3] For example, in the United States, the Glass-Steagall Act of 1933, which was effectively ignored for years until it was partially repealed by the Gramm-Leach-Bliley Act of 1999.

[4] Genspring Family Office is an independent U.S.-based multi-family office that provides investment advisory to wealthy individuals and families.

[5] When there is asymmetrical information, the professional knows more about the industry than the client does. As a result, the client is at a disadvantage and, if the professional does not act with integrity, is at risk of getting taken advantage of.

[6] Commissions and trailers should be forwarded to clients rather than rejected altogether because clients can save substantial money on fees in the process.

[7] Bernard, Tara. "Trusted Advisor or Stock Pusher? Finance Bill May not Settle It." New York Times, 2010.

[8] For example, a personal family office would cost, on the low end, $500,000 per year.

[9] According to Ontario Securities Commission (OSC), a Permitted Investor is a person with $5 million or more in investable assets.

Chapter 3

[1] It is useful to note here that an inefficient market is not inaccurate but just slow. In the long-term, prices will reflect the intrinsic value of investments despite market inefficiency. In the short-term, however, mispricing can persist long enough for investors to act on them and benefit in the process.

[2] "Herding" describes a psychological phenomenon in which people come to believe something based on the fact that others believe it to be true. We discuss herding in Chapter Nine along with the other heuristics which play a role in investing.

[3] GMO April 2012 Investor Letter

[4] This large difference in cumulative returns is a result of the "miracle" of compounding, which is discussed in Chapter Seven.

Chapter 4

[1] Absent of earnings growth and the opportunity cost of their capital.

[2] Marks, Howard. January 2, 2000 Memo: Bubble.com

[3] Marks, Howard. The Most Important Thing: Uncommon Sense For The Thoughtful Investor. New York: Columbia UP, 2011. p.33

Chapter 5

[1] Different types of securities include stocks and bonds, among many others.

[2] There are times when investors navigate market highs and lows based on looking at individual securities and only investing in undervalued ones. This important aspect of investing would fall into security selection because marketing timing refers to purely macroeconomic-based investing.

[3] Ibbotson, Roger G. and Paul D. Kaplan. "Does Asset Allocation Policy Explain 40, 90, or 100 Percent of Performance?" Financial Analysts Journal, 66:2.

[4] With transactions cost, it is a negative-sum game. That is why the study shows some sub groups with greater than 100% and other less than 100%. On average across all investors, asset allocation accounts for over 100% of returns.

[5] Ibbotson, Roger G. and Paul D. Kaplan. *Does Asset Allocation Policy Explain 40, 90, or 100 Percent of Performance?* Financial Analysts Journal Volume 66 • Number 2.

[6] Ibbotson SBBI Valuation Yearbook, 2010.

[7] Significant drawdowns for pure equity investors are unavoidable. For example, during the recession that took place in the early 1970's, even

Endnotes 187

Berkshire Hathaway's investment portfolio, managed by Warren Buffett, experienced a prolonged contraction of a third of its value. Of course, Buffet's persistence amidst falling stock prices paid tremendous dividends when the market rebounded. During the drawdown, however, Buffett himself was, despite his tremendous wealth, cash poor and earned a comparatively modest sum of $50,000 a year for several years. (Shroeder, Alice. The Snowball: Warren Buffett and the Business of Life). Few people of comparable wealth are willing and able to withstand such draw downs.

[8] For example, consider an investment of $100. A 20% decline brings the value down to $80. To return to $100, the investment must appreciate by $20, which is now 25% of the current value.

[9] Two to five percent of their overall net worth, meaning there are twenty to fifty positions. A "position" here may refer to an investment structure, such as a hedge fund, investing in many underlying securities.

Chapter 6

[1] Although investment managers are extremely important in the traditional asset classes, they generally can only legitimately strive to beat out the broader market by a few percentage points a year. Over the long term, these marginal out-performances can compound in significant gains (as we discuss in Chapter Seven), but the primary source of returns is still the power of the market rather than the power of the investment manager. This characteristic of Traditional assets may be clearer after reading the following section on Alternative assets, which offers a useful contrast.

[2] The important subject of intrinsic value is also discussed in Chapter Three.

[3] Reinhard, C.M. and Kenneth Rogoff. *This Time is Different: Eight Centuries of financial Folly*, 2009.

[4] The observant reader may pause at this point and ask, in light of the credit quality downgrade of the U.S. government by the S&P, why do credit instruments backed by the U.S. government still qualify for this category? Since the market clearly did not agree with the credit agencies, the downgrade has had little if any impact. Interest rates on Treasuries (amazingly) declined after the downgrade as people continued to treat them as a safe haven amidst their "flight to quality". As this section goes on to explain, the "flight to quality" effect is one of the key characteristics for securities to qualify for this asset class, which is used as protection against financial catastrophe.

[5] These three risks are, respectively, referred to as "credit risk", "liquidity risk", and "call risk".

[6] Swensen, David. *Pioneering Portfolio Management*. 2005

[7] Wheaton, William et al. *100 Years of Commercial Real Estate Prices in Manhattan*. Real Estate Economics, Vol 37.

[8] It is very important to note here that these are hypothetical asset allocations rather than recommendations for the amount that one should allocate to each strategy. Such decision making is particular to each investor, as we discuss in Chapter Two.

Chapter 7

[1] According to SPIVA (Standard and Poor's Indices v Active Funds) Report, 2010, only 7.45% of all Canadian active managers outperformed the S&P/TSX over the 5-year period between 2005-2009. In the U.S, only 9.2% of active funds outperformed the S&P 500 over the same period.

[2] These ideas are explained in much more depth in Chapter Three

[3] This topic is discussed in Chapter Six

[4] As of this writing, clients are expected to get the vast majority, if not the entirety, of their assets retuned from the trustee managing MF Global's bankruptcy but have been subject to months of lock-ups. Several months since MF's bankruptcy, many clients are yet to get back the majority of their assets.

[5] In various forms of private equity and certain types of real estate this may not be as relevant, but then other update sources should be sought out.

[6] To put this figure into perspective, the S&P 500 price-to-earnings ratio was almost always between 10 and 20 from 1920 to 1990.

Chapter 8

[1] Goldstein, Paul. "How Secure are Canadian Life Insurance Policies." 2009.

[2] Please note there may be adverse tax consequences if any of these actions is taken without careful consideration as to how such consequences are avoided.

[3] Insurance premiums that are paid by a corporation, while not deductible for tax purposes in the corporation, can be used to erode the corporation's taxable surplus. That is, retained earnings of the corporation, which if paid out via salary or dividend, would be taxable in the hands of the recipient. The insurance premiums erode that surplus and the death proceeds that come into the corporation are tax-free to the corporation and can usually be paid out to shareholders, totally, tax free.

Chapter 9

[1] Many of the ideas in this chapter were drawn from a speech made by Charlie Munger at Harvard Law School (1995), entitled *The Psychology of Human Misjudgment.*

[2] Goldstein NJ, Martin SJ, Cialdini RB. Yes 50 Secrets from the
Science of Persuasion. London: Profile Books, 2007

[3] Dennis T. Regan, "Effects of a Favor and Liking on Compliance," Journal of Experimental Social Psychology, Vol. 7 (1971), pp. 627–639.

[4] Sweetening the Till: The Use of Candy to Increase Restaurant Tipping; David B. Strohmetz, Bruce Rind, Monmouth University Temple University; Reed Fisher, Michael Lynn, Johnson State College Cornell University, in (2002) Journal of Applied Social Psychology, 32, 300-309.

[5] The sunk cost fallacy is the bias which prompts us to continue with a venture once an investment of time, money, or any other resources has been made, when (instead) we should have cut our losses and moved on.

[6] Ryan Spellecy (2003). "Reviving Ulysses contracts". Kennedy Institute of Ethics Journal 13 (4): 373–392. DOI:10.1353/ken.2004.0010. PMID 15049305.

[7] Skinner designed a chamber to measure responses of mice and pigeons, and their responses to changes in their environment. With this chamber he proved that how these mice and pigeons responded to certain situations was greatly correlated with the timing, sizing, and measure of the consequences. As a simple example, if a mouse would receive a pellet of food by pulling a lever, it would begin regularly pulling that lever.

[8] As opposed to fixed schedule reinforcement, where an incentive is provided in a predictable pattern.

[9] Langer, Ellen J. (1975), "The Illusion of Control," Journal of Personality and Social Psychology 32 (2): 311–328.

[10] Svenson, O. (1981). Are we less risky and more skillful than our fellow drivers? Acta Psychologica, 47, 143-151.

[11] DALBAR, Quantitative Analysis of Investor Behavior (QAIB) April 2012.

[12] Zweig, Jason (November 19, 2009), "How to Ignore the Yes-Man in Your Head," Wall Street Journal (Dow Jones & Company), retrieved 2010-06-13.

[13] 37 people, who all saw each other, witnessed a murder in Kew Gardens, NY on March 13, 1964, and not a single witness called the police or attempted to save her.

[14] Ariely, D., Loewenstein, G. and D. Prelec, 2003, Coherent arbitrariness: Stable demand curves without stable preferences, Quarterly Journal of Economics 118, 73-105.

[15] For example, the period between 1995 and 1998, where the S&P 500 generated returns of +37, +23, +33, and +28, respectively.

[16] During this period, businesses proved entirely unreliable and government-backed securities were the only island of stability. Consequently, this generation became exceedingly partial towards bonds.

[17] Buehler, Roger; Dale Griffin, Michael Ross (1994). "Exploring the "planning fallacy": Why people underestimate their task completion times". Journal of Personality and Social Psychology (American Psychological Association) 67 (3): 366–381. DOI:10.1037/0022-3514.67.3.366.

[18] In this experiment, Cialdini instructed students to first place one hand in a bucket of hot water, then the other hand in a bucket of room temperature water. The students reported that the room temperature water felt cold. He repeated the experiment, but changed the hot water to cold water. Again, after the students felt the cold water they reported feeling that the room temperature water was hot.

[19] Influence: The Psychology of Persuasion . By Robert B. Cialdini, Ph.D. (Quill, NY, 1984. Revised 1993).

[20] It might be a common story in other religions and cultures as well, as I have also heard it in the context of a Buddhist monk.

[21] McNeil, B.J., Pauker, S.G., Sox, H.C., Tversky, A. On the elicitation of preferences for alternative therapies. New England Journal of Medicine. 1982 May 27; 306(21):1259-62. PMID: 7070445.

[22] Milgram, S. Dynamics of obedience. Washington: National Science Foundation, 25 January 1961. (Mimeo)

[23] Ginnett, R. C. (1993). Crews as groups: Their formation and their leadership. In E. L. Wiener, B. G. Kanki, & R. L. Helmreich (Eds.), Cockpit resource management (pp. 71-98). San Diego, CA: Academic Press.

[24] Driskell, J. E., & Webster, M. (1985). Status generalization. In J. Berger & M. Zelditch (Eds.), Status, rewards, and influence (pp. 108-141). San Francisco: Jossey-Bass.

[25] "The Stanford Prison Experiment". http://documentaryheaven.com/the-stanford-prison-experiment/ Retrieved 7/23/2012.

Chrysler
Corkison

— 416/885 7233

Erin ~~////~~ Tues/12:00 ~~26~~th Room #302

~~Akron~~